LANGUAGE

Understanding the grammar

MĀORI LANGUAGE

Understanding the grammar

Te Reo Māori
He Whakamārama Wetenga Reo

by

David Kārena-Holmes

Published by Reed Books, a division of Reed Publishing (NZ) Ltd,
39 Rawene Rd, Birkenhead, Auckland.
Associated companies, branches and representatives
throughout the world.

ISBN 0 7900 0572 7

First published 1995 by D.M. Kārena-Holmes
New edition 1997 Reed Publishing (NZ) Ltd

Printed in New Zealand

To

Shirley Kārena

'Ko Hine-tītama koe, matawai ana
te whatu i te tirohanga.'

Foreword

The very word 'grammar' conjures up a dull, dusty approach to learning a language. Yet to master any language a knowledge of grammar is essential, whether implicit or explicit.

There is no easy way to master a language except through 'toil and trouble', that is, constant application and practice. Mistakes inevitably will be made, but from those mistakes comes progress and eventual fluency.

Constant repetition of phrases, as in the audio-lingual method, certainly helps one acquire the pattern of the language, but sooner or later the enquiring student will have to ask why we say something one way and not another. Just as we need rules to live by, so do we need rules to learn a language. It is at this juncture that a knowledge of grammar becomes important.

As David Kārena-Holmes states, 'confusion reigns with regard to points of Māori grammar, and this is exacerbated by a lack of standardisation of terminology'. Any book that helps people to speak a language better is to be applauded, and the timely re-publication of *Maori Language* is valuable grist to our language acquisition mill.

Rāwiri, hei konei noa ka puta he mihi ki a koe mō hēmanawa i pā, mō tōhau i heke, mō tuarā i pahore engari ia anei tōna whakatinanatanga ko te pukapuka nei.

Mā konei pea e ekea ai nga kōtihitihi o te reo e wawatatia nei e te hunga whai mai i tō taua reo.

Kia ora rawa atu koe.

Tīmoti Kāretu
Māori Language Commissioner

Contents

Note: *A Dictionary of the Maori Language* by Herbert W. Williams has been referred to throughout simply as William's dictionary. The macron has been used to indicate long vowels in Maori words, except where it is not used in original book-titles (e.g. *Let's Learn Maori* and *Ngaa Mahi Whakaari a Tiitokowaru*)

Preface

English language grammars of Māori effectively begin with *A Grammar and Vocabulary of the Language of New Zealand* published by the Church Missionary Society in London in 1820.* It was not until a century and a half later, however, that a grammar properly descriptive of Māori could be considered to be fully fledged — in Bruce Biggs' *Let's Learn Maori*, first published in 1969 (revised edition 1973) which presented 'an entirely different grammatical theory' resulting in 'a much simplified system of classification' of words.†

This present book — substantially a re-write, and expansion, of *Grammar Basics: English-Māori* (1993) — is based, like its predecessor, upon the principles established in *Let's Learn Maori* as I have understood them (any faults of interpretation are my own).

This book is intended as an aid to English-speaking learners of Māori. It is not intended to be, in itself, a course in learning Māori, but a supplementary reference, or guidebook, to accompany such learning. Its particular focus is upon how Māori differs from English in terms of the functions of words and of how they are used to construct phrases and sentences.

It should be well enough known that there are several differences of dialect in Māori. Whilst some references are made to such differences, the focus of this book is really upon the grammatical principles which are common to all dialects.

Such principles or rules may be thought of, perhaps, as forming a net. Some fish will escape through the mesh, or through unnoticed holes. Although some kind of reasonable comprehensiveness (at a basic level) has been aimed for, it cannot be claimed that the rules outlined here (or any rules) can cover all possible forms of expression in Māori.

(If more detail on particular points should be required, it may be sought in the material suggested in the 'Further Reading' sections with

* Thomas Kendall, who came as a missionary to the Bay of Islands in 1814, is credited with collecting most of the material for this book. Two young chiefs, Tui and Titere, in England in 1818, also supplied material to Samuel Lee of Cambridge University. The book was completed in collaboration when Hongi Hika, Waikato and Kendall visited England in 1820. See Judith Binney's *The Legacy of Guilt — A Life of Thomas Kendall* (Auckland, 1968).

† *Let's Learn Maori*, p. 51.

which many of the chapters finish.)

What should be emphasized here is that this book is addressed from one learner to other learners. Indeed, my only justification for writing this book is that of being, myself, but a learner of Māori seeking further understanding of the language — and I am sure that there must be many ways yet to be developed of further simplifying and clarifying the presentation of the essentials of Māori grammar. The assumption here is that, for English-speaking learners of Māori, an understanding of the basics of the grammar can certainly be useful. But this is always provided that this kind of 'understanding' does not become a substitute for practice — with fluent native speakers (the only true authorities) wherever and whenever possible.

The survival of Māori as a living language depends not upon how many people understand the grammar, but upon how many actually use the language as their preferred means of expression, in both speech and writing.

David Kārena-Holmes
October 1995

The resetting of this book for publication by Reed Books has allowed for some minor emendations to be made to the text. It also provides the opportunity for the reiteration of my conviction that there are only three requirements for the acquisition of fluency in Māori — firstly, practice; secondly, practice; and thirdly, practice.

Nō reira, he mihi nui, he mihi aroha, ki te hunga ora, ki te hunga mate, ki ngā kaikōrero rātou ko ngā ākonga o tēnei reo rangatira, he tāonga tuku iho nō ngā tūpuna o te iwi Māori. Ka mihi ake anō ahau ki a Tīmoti Kāretu mō āna kupu whakataki, ki a Ratu Tibble mō tāna āwhina, ki te ētitā hoki o te tuhinga nei, arā, ki a Joanna Elliott.

D.K-H.
July 1997

Introduction

The differences between the Māori and English languages are not merely those of a different vocabulary. They are differences in the actual functions of some types of words, and in the manner in which words are linked into meaningful phrases and sentences.

Certain types of words are used in Māori, for instance, which have no counterpart in English. And, conversely, certain types of English words have no counterpart in Māori. Even where a degree of word correspondence exists, the word-order in Māori is often different from that of English.

These differences mean that the grammar used for English will not necessarily be suitable for Māori.

Māori can indeed be quite confusing to the speaker of English unless there is a clear understanding of the principles underlying the function of particular words in Māori, and of exactly how phrases and sentences are constructed in Māori (as opposed to how they are constructed in English).

When, however, these principles are clearly understood, on their own terms, the basic grammar of Māori will even be found, in several respects, to be simpler, and more logical than that of English.

Such an understanding may be most effectively acquired by beginning, so to speak, 'from the beginning' — by going back to some of the most fundamental principles of grammar.

CHAPTER I

Base Words and Particles

In any human language, BASE WORDS are the words that carry most of the weight of meaning in any sentence.

For example, the base words are shown in bold print in the following sentence:

In the **beginning God created** the **heaven** and the **earth**.

Most of the essential meaning of the sentence would be reasonably well conveyed simply by the base words on their own:

. . . beginning God created . . . heaven . . . earth

The smaller words (in the above example, 'in', 'the' and 'and') which connect the base words and help to form a fluent sentence are called PARTICLES.

Particles do not have meaning in the same sense that base words may be said to have meaning. Particles are words which have a grammatical function and convey certain kinds of secondary information.

As a simple example in Māori,* the well-known greeting

*Kia **ora**!*

may be described as a single phrase, consisting of the base word ***ora*** (which has the meaning of 'to be alive and healthy') preceded by the particle *kia*, which expresses the idea that the speaker 'wishes that something is in fact the case'. In other words, an appropriate, literal, translation of *Kia **ora**!* would be 'I hope you are well.' or simply 'Be well!'

* In this book, in the Māori text, all base words are shown in bold print.

† That is, to move oneself, not to move some other object. For further explanation of the terms 'transitive' and 'intransitive' see ch. 24

The equally familiar call of welcome

Haere *mai!*

consists of the base word ***haere*** followed by the direction particle *mai*. The basic meaning of ***haere*** is 'to move' (in an intransitive† sense) and, commonly, it has the sense of 'to go'. The particle *mai*, however, expresses the idea of 'in the direction of the speaker' (almost exactly the same sense as the somewhat out-of-date English word 'hither'). In other words, a literal translation of ***Haere*** *mai!* would be 'Move hither!' or 'Come here!' (The sense in Māori is that of a highly courteous welcome.)

Particles, such as *kia* and *mai*, are used continuously in Māori speech and text, as in the following examples (some flexibility must be allowed in translation):

Kia ***kaha!***	(Be strong!)
Kia ***tūpato!***	(Be careful!)
Titiro *mai.*	(Look over here.)
Karanga *mai!*	(Call in this direction!)

There are thousands of base words in Māori (and new words are being added as well) but there are only about 60* particles.

* See Note 1, p. 118.

CHAPTER 2

The Construction of Phrases in Māori

Almost every phrase in Māori contains a base word, or more than one base word, carrying the main meaning part of the phrase. Sometimes a phrase will consist solely of a single base word. More often the base word or words will have a particle or particles in front, or after, or in both places.

The following sentence is separated into phrases (base words are shown in bold print; all other words are particles):

Ka ***whakakitea*** *mai* was shown	*e* ***ia*** by him	*ki* ***ahau*** to me
he ***awa wai*** ora a river water life	***pīata*** tonu clear	me te ***karāihe*** as (the) crystal
e ***puta*** mai ana emerging	i te ***torōna*** from the throne	o te ***Atua.*** of (the) God.

(That is: 'He showed me a river of the water of life, clear as crystal, emerging from the throne of God.')

The above example shows that in some phrases Māori requires particles where English doesn't (e.g. *e* ***puta*** *mai ana* — 'emerging') and in other cases doesn't require particles where English does (e.g. *he* ***awa wai ora*** — 'a river of water of life'). It shows that while English meanings can be given to all the base words, only some of the particles need be translated into English, and others simply don't have any English translation.

What is illustrated, then, is a variety of simple phrase-patterns in Māori, which may serve as examples for the points mentioned in the paragraph at the beginning of this chapter, as follows:

(a) Every phrase in Māori contains at least one base word — e.g. *Ka* ***whakakitea*** *mai*

(b) or more than one base word —

e.g. *he* ***awa wai ora***

(c) often with a particle or particles in front —
e.g. *e* ***ia*** *and* *me te* ***karāihe***

(d) or after —
e.g. ***pīata*** *tonu*

(e) or in both places —
e.g. *Ka* ***whakakitea*** *mai* *and* *e* ***puta*** *mai ana*

Often, of course (but not illustrated above) a phrase may consist of simply a single base word, as in the second phrase of the following sentence:

Me ***haere***	***tātou***.	
Ought to go	we.	(We ought to go.)

Here, the single base word ***tātou*** (we/us) forms the complete subject phrase of the sentence. (In the first phrase the base ***haere*** is preceded by the particle *me* which, as a verbal particle, expresses the idea that something 'should or ought to be done'.

The principle upon which this book is based is that the first step towards understanding the structure of Māori consists of learning to distinguish the phrase-patterns of the language, simply by firstly identifying which words are base words and which are particles.

This involves learning to recognise each of the common particles, and learning the different kinds of information that each one may supply.

With base words, on the other hand, it is the various meanings which may be learnt (and a vocabulary may gradually be built up).

Because there are comparatively few particles, and because they are used so repeatedly, it should be possible to acquire familiarity at least with the common uses of most of them within a reasonable period of time.

No-one, however, should be expected to know the meaning of every base word in Māori (just as no-one is expected to know the meaning of every word in English). But what can be of great advantage in coping with base words is to have an understanding of the few classes or types to which they may be seen to belong — particularly because these types and their functions are not the same in Māori as in English.

CHAPTER 3

Main Types of Base Words and their Functions

In all languages there are thousands of base words, but they may be seen to be of only a few different types, or 'parts of speech', according to their different functions in a sentence. These types, however, are not the same in all languages.

The aim of this short chapter is to attempt to clarify exactly how the types of base words in Māori differ from those of English.

Briefly, in English, a word is called a NOUN when it gives a name to a thing, a person, or a place. Words such as 'house', 'woman', 'Dunedin' are nouns.

A word is called a VERB when it expresses an action or a state of being. Words such as 'sit', 'go', 'sing' are verbs which express action. Words such as 'seem' and 'be' are verbs which express states of being.

A word is called an ADJECTIVE when it describes a thing, usually named by a noun. Words such as 'good', 'red', 'careful' are adjectives.

These three types of words (NOUN, VERB, ADJECTIVE) are the main types of base words in English.*

But not in Māori.

Māori has base words that give names to things, and which therefore may be called NOUNS (but the categories of nouns in Māori are different to those of English).

Māori has base words that express actions, and which therefore may be called VERBS (but verbs expressing states of being form a whole separate class of verbs in Māori).

Māori does not, however, have any specific type of word which should be called an ADJECTIVE.

Regarding ADVERBS see p. 24, and Note 2, p. 118.

Since several books currently available (including the indispensable Williams' dictionary) still refer to some Māori words as being 'adjectives' perhaps further explanation on this point should be offered here.

The reason why Māori words such as ***pai*** ('to be good'†) and ***tūpato*** ('to be careful') should be regarded as VERBS (rather than adjectives) is not hard to find.

It has already been mentioned that verbs are base words which express either 'actions' or 'states of being'. Almost all verbs in English are 'action' verbs. There are very few 'being' verbs in English. By far the most important 'being' verb in English is the verb 'to be' itself. This is the verb which has forms such as the following:

PRESENT TENSE

SINGULAR	PLURAL
I **am**	we **are**
you **are**	you **are**
he/she/it **is**	they **are**

In the simple past tense there are the forms 'I was', 'you were' etc. and in the future tense 'I will be' etc. as well as other tenses such as 'have been', 'had been' and 'If (I/you etc.) were . . .' and so on.

This verb 'to be' is very widely used in English. One of its common uses is to form sentences with adjectives, as in (for example)

'The house is red.'

and 'We are careful.'

In Māori there is no equivalent of this verb 'to be'. Instead, Māori has a great number (in contrast to the small number in English) of VERBS expressing 'states of being'.

For example, the word ***pai*** is not an adjective meaning 'good', but a verb meaning 'to be good'. The word ***whero*** is not an adjective meaning 'red', but a verb meaning 'to be red'. The word ***tūpato*** is not an adjective meaning 'careful', but a verb meaning 'to be careful'.

† Here, *pai* is considered separately from the action verb *pai (-ngia)* — 'to like'.

This is clearly confirmed when a comparison is made between such examples as the following:

(a) *Ka **oma*** *te **kurī**.*
runs the dog (The dog runs.)

Here ***oma*** is a verb, similar in meaning to the English verb 'runs'.

(b) *Ka **pai*** *te **kurī**.*
is good the dog (The dog is good.)

Here ***pai*** is a verb, similar in meaning to the whole English verbal phrase 'is good'.

Because there is a great number of 'being' verbs in Māori, they may be considered to form a separate class of base word. Accordingly, verbs of the ***oma*** type (which express 'actions') may be referred to as ACTION VERBS, and those of the ***pai, whero*** or ***tūpato*** type (which express 'states of being') are called STATIVE* VERBS (or simply, for short, STATIVES).

The stative verbs of Māori do not, of course, replace the English verb 'to be' in all situations. Nor is it implied that there must always be, in Māori, some form of verbal counterpart for the English 'to be', or any other verb.

In English, a sentence must, properly, contain a verb — even if only the copula verb 'to be'. e.g. 'This is the house.'
In Māori, sentences may be quite complete without any verb.

e.g. *Ko **tēnei*** *te **whare**.*
This the house (This is the house.)

The three main types of base words in Maōri may therefore be said to be
NOUNS • ACTION VERBS • STATIVE VERBS

* This term was originally coined to classify words of similar function in Hebrew.

CHAPTER 4

Further Differences in Base Words between English and Māori

In order to avoid the sort of confusion which can make the learning of Māori much more difficult than it need be, the whole system of base words in Māori should be clearly differentiated from that of English.

Brief consideration of a few features of English may serve for purposes of comparison:

The main types of base words in English are

NOUNS • VERBS (Both 'action' and 'being') • ADJECTIVES

A great many words in English can, however, belong to more than one type. The word 'fish', for example, may be a noun (as in 'He caught a fish.') or a verb (as in 'We are going to fish for trout.'). Also, many different alterations can be made to words in English. Some of these alterations change words from one type to another.

For example, PREFIXES, such as 'im-', 'in-' and 'un-' may be added to words to form an opposite sense to that of the original word.

e.g. 'possible' → 'impossible'
'do' → 'undo'

And SUFFIXES, such as '-ish' and '-like' may be added to nouns to form adjectives.

e.g. 'child' (noun) → 'childish' (adjective)
→ 'childlike' (adjective)

On the other hand, the SUFFIX '-ness' may be added to adjectives to form nouns.

e.g. 'bright' (adjective) → 'brightness' (noun)
'childish' (adjective) → 'childishness' (noun)

Almost any English adjective can be transformed into another type of describing word called an ADVERB* simply by adding the suffix '-ly'

e.g. 'slow' (adjective) → 'slowly' (adverb)

Many words in English, in fact, have forms for noun, verb, adjective and adverb.

e.g. 'beauty', 'beautify', 'beautiful' and 'beautifully'.

Within a single type of base word, even, there may be numerous forms deriving from a single root word.

e.g. the following nouns related to the word 'clear' — 'clarification', 'clarity', 'clearance', 'clearing', 'clearness'.

The foregoing few examples give some indication of the complexity of English. It is a complexity, however, with which anyone who has fully acquired English as a first language has probably become so familiar that it scarcely requires thinking about in ordinary, daily use of the language. The complex patterns of word usage in English may even be simply accepted as the normal, basic patterns of language in general.

But they aren't. The patterns (and complexities) of English belong to English. They may be parallelled to a large extent in other, closely related languages, but they have far fewer parallels in Māori. Most of the complexity of English is quite irrelevant (and may even be a hindrance) to the learning of Māori.

It might even be said that the greatest difficulty for English-speakers in learning Māori is that of knowing English first!

This means that, whilst notice may be taken of certain features in common between the languages, it can only be of advantage to have as clear and full an understanding as possible of the main differences between English and Māori — particularly differences at the most fundamental level.

* See Note 2, p. 118.

The main types of base words in Māori are —

NOUNS • ACTION VERBS • STATIVE VERBS

In common with English, Māori has many words which can be used as both verbs and nouns.

For example, the word ***kai*** may function either as an action verb (with a meaning similar to the English verb 'eat') or as a noun (with a meaning similar to the English word 'food'). Sometimes there are even parallels with English. For example, the word ***mahi*** (to work) may also be used as a noun (*te **mahi*** — 'the work').

But because a particular word in English can be either a noun or a verb is no indication that the Māori translation for one or the other can be similarly used.

The English word 'fish', for example, can be used (as has previously been mentioned) as either noun or verb. But the Māori word ***ika*** (fish) is used only as a noun. A quite different word such as ***hī*** (to fish with a line) or ***hao*** (to fish with a net) is required for the verb.

Because a word is of a certain type in one language does not mean that its translation is necessarily of the same type. The word 'what' may be a pronoun, noun, adverb, interjection, conjunction and adjective in English — yet its Māori translation, ***aha***, is primarily an action verb in Māori (meaning 'doing what?').

The word 'evening' is a noun in English, but its Māori translation, ***ahiahi*** (while it may be used as a noun) is a stative verb in the sentence *Ka **ahiahi***. — '(It) became evening.'

The question arises then — should words such as ***kai, mahi*** and ***ahiahi*** be considered primarily as nouns or verbs or both?

Because there are nouns (e.g. ***whare, ika, rākau***) which are not used as verbs, it seems simpler to consider all words which are used as verbs as being primarily verbs.

To this it may be added that —

all action verbs and many stative verbs may be used also as nouns
and that —

base words of all three main types may be used as describing words (that is, as adjectives).

Such a system avoids a lot of confusion — and, in fact, discovers Māori to be in some ways much simpler than English.

Such alterations as do occur in Māori words are certainly not nearly as numerous, various or complicated as those which occur in English.

CHAPTER 5

Summarizing So Far

In Māori, almost every phrase consists of one or more base words, carrying the main meaning of the phrase. Sometimes a base word will stand on its own in a phrase. More often the base word or words will have a particle or particles before, after, or in both places.

Being able to identify and distinguish the base words and particles in a phrase is of great help in understanding the construction of Māori phrases and sentences.

There may be considered to be three main types, or classes, of base words in Māori:

NOUNS • ACTION VERBS • STATIVE VERBS

All action verbs, and many stative verbs, may be used as nouns (sometimes 'noun-endings' are added).*

Base words of all three main types may, without alteration, be used as adjectives.†

Each of the three main types of base word in Māori (nouns, action verbs and stative verbs) is considered separately in some further detail (and further contrasts with English illustrated) in, respectively, Chapters 7, 27 and 28.

But firstly, it may be useful, as a model of comparison between the languages, to turn to the small but very important set of base words — a sub-class of nouns — known as PERSONAL PRONOUNS.

* See Chap. 8.
+ See Chap. 9.

CHAPTER 6

Base Words 1: The Personal Pronouns

PRONOUNS are words that are used in place of nouns, often to avoid repetition of the noun. They may be considered, perhaps, a sub-class of personal nouns.

In English, pronouns such as 'it' and 'this' are used for things, and pronouns such as 'I', 'you' and 'we' are used for people. The group of pronouns used for referring to people are called the PERSONAL PRONOUNS. In the learning of Māori (or any other language) probably one of the first priorities should be to master this particular group of words — the personal pronouns.

The personal pronouns of Māori are not any more complicated than those of English, but different distinctions (to those of English) are made with them. To illustrate what is meant by this, here is a scheme of the personal pronouns in English:

	SINGULAR		PLURAL	
	Subject	Object	Subject	Object
1st person	I	me	we	us
2nd person	you	you	you	you
3rd person	he/she	him/her	they	them

It may be seen that English distinguishes —

(a) SUBJECT from OBJECT (that is — in all cases but the second person — there is a different form of pronoun for the subject of a sentence from that for the object)

(b) GENDER, in the 3rd person singular ('he' from 'she' and 'him' from 'her')
(c) only 2 NUMBERS (singular and plural)
(d) only 3 PERSONS (1st, 2nd and 3rd persons).

Māori, by contrast, does not distinguish subject from object, nor does it distinguish gender. Instead, however, Māori distinguishes —

(a) 3 NUMBERS (one person, two people and 3 or more people)
(b) 4 PERSONS (1st person INCLUSIVE, 1st person EXCLUSIVE, 2nd person and 3rd person).

The scheme of personal pronouns in Māori is therefore as follows:

FORMS FOR SUBJECT OR OBJECT			
	1 person	2 people	3 or more
1st person inclusive		we/us ***tāua***	we/us ***tātou***
1st person exclusive	I/me ***au** or **ahau***	we/us ***māua***	we/us ***mātou***
2nd person	you ***koe***	you ***kōrua***	you ***koutou***
3rd person	he/she/him/her ***ia***	they/them ***rāua***	they/them ***rātou***

It seems to be often the distinction in the 1st person, between inclusive and exclusive, which causes most problems for speakers of English.

INCLUSIVE and EXCLUSIVE refer to whether or not the person or people spoken to is/are included or excluded in the reference.

Since the person or people spoken to, in any situation is/are always the 2ND PERSON this means that the INCLUSIVE form is a combination of the 1st and 2nd PERSONS. Whereas the EXCLUSIVE form is a combination of the 1st and 3rd PERSONS. That is:

au	+	***koe***	=	***tāua***	(INCLUSIVE)
au	+	***ia***	=	***māua***	(EXCLUSIVE)
au	+	***kōrua*** *or* ***koutou***	=	***tātou***	(INCLUSIVE)
au	+	***rāua*** *or* ***rātou***	=	***mātou***	(EXCLUSIVE)

As far as the use of the personal pronouns in Māori is concerned, it needs to be carefully noted that when speaking of more than one person the pronoun embracing all the people being mentioned is used.

That is, for the equivalent of 'you (singular) and I' one does not say ***koe*** *me** ***au***, but ***tāua*** ('the two of us'). For 'you (plural) and I' one says ***tātou*** ('all of us').

For 'Mary and I' one does not say ***Mere*** *me* ***au***, but ***māua*** *ko*† ***Mere*** (which has the sense of 'the two of us — the person other than myself being Mary'). Similarly, for 'Hata, Mary and I' one would say ***mātou*** *ko* ***Hata*** *ko* ***Mere***.

For 'you (singular) and James' one would not say ***koe*** *me* ***Hēmi***, but ***kōrua*** *ko* ***Hēmi***. For 'you (plural) and James', one would say ***koutou*** *ko* ***Hēmi***.

In the 3rd person, the appropriate pronoun is placed after the first name. Thus: 'Mary and James' is rendered ***Mere rāua*** *ko* ***Hēmi***. 'Hata, Mary and James' is ***Hata rātou*** *ko* ***Mere*** *ko* ***Hēmi***.

As another example of this use, for 'my friend and I' one would say ***māua*** *ko tōku* ***hoa***.

There are two other personal pronouns of importance in Māori:

(1) ***wai*** (who) — commonly used in questions such as *Ko* ***wai ia***? (Who is he/she?) but it should be noted that whereas in English we ask 'What is your name?' in Māori the question is *Ko* ***wai*** *tōu* ***ingoa***?

(2) ***mea*** — this word, also used for a 'thing', may be used as an 'indefinite' personal pronoun (so-and-so).

The entries in Williams' dictionary for both these words should be checked.

* *me* = 'and' (in some situations). See p. 49.

† For *ko* see p. 48.

The word ***ahau*** appears to be freely interchangeable with ***au***. Other, less common, variants of this pronoun are ***awau*** and ***awahau***. In dialects of Tūhoe and Ngāti Porou the first and third person pronouns for three or more people are commonly given endings in ***-au*** rather than ***-ou*** — thus: ***tātau, mātau, rātau.***

Although there is no difference in the form of the pronoun for subject or object, it will be found that when a personal pronoun is the object of a sentence it is normally, in most constructions, directly preceded by the PERSONAL ARTICLE, a*. This article has no counterpart in English.

e.g. ***Hōmai***	*te* ***rākau***	*ki a*	***au.***
Give	the stick	to	me.

This is in accordance with the rule that, after any of the LOCATION PREPOSITIONS, *ki, kei, i* or *hei* (see Chap. 12) both personal nouns and personal pronouns are preceded by *a*, and, in Māori, the object is, in most constructions, introduced by either *ki* or *i* (see Chap. 24).
The exception to this rule is that the *a* is not used before ***ahau*** (or the variants ***awau*** and ***awahau***).

e.g. ***Hōmai***	*te* ***rākau***	*ki*	***ahau.***
Give	the stick	to	me.

That there is no distinction between subject and object in the pronouns in Māori may be taken as convenient compared with English — considering the frequency with which subject and object forms are confused in English. (e.g. For a sentence such as 'Mary and I went to town.' one will frequently hear 'Mary and me' or 'Me and Mary'.)

Similarly, that the pronoun ***ia*** does not specify male or female is very convenient. Consider the problem encountered in English in such a conversation as the following:

'I've been to visit my friend.'
'Oh — who is he? — or she?'

* See p. 47

This kind of gender dilemma does not exist in Māori, and God can be referred to as ***Ia*** without any charge of sexism!

Further Reading

Most course material on Māori offers a range of practice exercises on the personal pronouns. The book *Te Rangatahi Elementary 1* provides an excellent series of visual aids in the form of cartoon illustrations, as well as examples of pronoun use on pp. 3, 14-16 and 53-55.

CHAPTER 7

Base Words 2: Nouns — Common Nouns, Personal Nouns and Location Nouns

In English nouns are traditionally separated into two types: COMMON NOUNS and PROPER NOUNS.

COMMON NOUNS

A common noun is a noun which gives a name to any of a class of things, people, or places. Thus, words such as 'tree', 'house', 'woman' and 'town' are COMMON NOUNS.

A great number of words classified as common nouns in English may also be used as VERBS (e.g. 'fish', 'walk', 'handle', 'book' etc.).

PROPER NOUNS

A proper noun is a noun which gives an individual name to a particular thing, person or place. Usually, a proper noun is identified in print by an initial capital letter.

Thus, words such as 'Olveston' (name of a house), 'Mary' and 'Dunedin'are PROPER NOUNS.

This English division into COMMON NOUNS and PROPER NOUNS doesn't work for Māori.

The main differences are —

(a) In Māori there are nouns of a particular type which have no counterpart in English. These are nouns which refer to locations, in space or time, and are therefore called Location Nouns.

(b) The English category of proper nouns must be split. Place-names, in Māori, belong with the above-mentioned Location Nouns. (This applies whether the actual name is Māori or any other language. e.g. ***Rotorua***, Dunedin etc.) Personal names (including names of things such as houses and canoes which are given personal names) become Personal Nouns.

(c) Words classified as COMMON NOUNS in Māori (unlike many of their English translations) are only words which do not function as verbs.

This means that, in Māori, there are three types of noun:
COMMON NOUNS, PERSONAL NOUNS and LOCATION NOUNS.

COMMON NOUNS

These words (like English common nouns) give names to any of a class of things, people or places. (Excluded, however, are those names of places which belong to the small group of LOCATION NOUNS described below.)

Thus, words such as ***rākau*** (tree, stick), ***manu*** (bird), ***ika*** (fish), ***whare*** (house, building), ***kōtiro*** (girl), ***kōwhatu*** (stone), and ***tonga*** (south) are COMMON NOUNS.

Very few common nouns in Māori show any difference between singular and plural. (They are almost all like the words 'deer' and 'sheep' in English.) The few words (listed below) which do show a change are all nouns referring to people, and for all except ***tamaiti*** (child) the change is simply in the lengthening of a vowel-sound:

SINGULAR		PLURAL
matua	parent	***mātua***
taina	younger sister	***tāina***
or	of a female or	or
teina	younger brother of a male	***tēina***
tuakana	older sister of a female	***tuākana***
	or older brother of a male	
tuahine	sister of a male	***tuāhine***
tipuna	ancestor	***tīpuna***
or		or
tupuna		***tūpuna***
wahine	woman/women	***wāhine***
tangata	person/people	***tāngata***
tamaiti	child/children	***tamariki***

The word ***tungāne*** (brother of a female) does not change.
COMMON NOUNS in Māori are usually directly preceded by —
either the INDEFINITE ARTICLE *he*

e.g. *he* ***manu*** — a bird or some birds

or by some form of DEFINITIVE

e.g. *ēnei* ***ika*** — these fish
tōku ***whare*** — my house

COMMON NOUNS, however, can be placed directly after* another NOUN or a VERB to add some DESCRIPTION.

e.g. *he* ***whare kōwhatu*** — a stone house

PERSONAL NOUNS

The personal names of people (e.g. Rangi, Kiri, Pita) are PERSONAL NOUNS. Houses, canoes, weapons and other things, including the months of the year, are also given individual names which are PERSONAL NOUNS (e.g. Mataatua, Horouta).

PERSONAL NOUNS in Māori are usually directly preceded by —
either the PERSONAL ARTICLE *a*

e.g. *Ka* ***haere*** *a* ***Mere****.* (Mary goes.)

or a PREPOSITION

e.g. *Ko* ***Rewi*** *te* ***rangatira****.* (Rewi is the chief.)
Mā ***Mere*** *tēnei* ***ika****.* (This fish is for Mary.)

PERSONAL NOUNS share a characteristic exclusively with the PERSONAL PRONOUNS† in that they are directly preceded by the PERSONAL ARTICLE, *a*, after any of the LOCATION PREPOSITIONS *ki*, *kei*, *i* or *hei*. This article has no counterpart in English.

* The nouns ***tino*** (essentiality) and ***āhua*** (appearance) are exceptions in that when used descriptively they are placed BEFORE the words they qualify.
e.g. ***tino pai*** (very good) ***āhua pai*** (only fairly good). The noun ***tupuna*** (ancestor) also can be placed BEFORE, in the phrase *te* ***tupuna whare*** (the ancestral house).

† The personal nouns and the personal pronouns are defined, collectively, as a single distinct class of base word — the Personals — in *Let's Learn Maori.*

e.g. ***Hoatu*** *te* ***rākau*** *ki a* ***Mere.***
Give the stick to Mary.

e.g. ***Hōmai*** *te* ***rākau*** *ki a* ***au.***
Give the stick to me.

PERSONAL NOUNS (this rule does not apply to the personal pronouns) are also preceded by *a* when they are the unemphasized subject of a sentence.

e.g. *Ka* ***haere*** *a* ***Mere.*** (Mary goes.)

The rules governing the use of the personal article are re-stated on p. 47.

Where they are not preceded by the personal article, PERSONAL NOUNS are usually preceded by a PREPOSITION.

e.g. Ko ***Rewi*** te ***hoa*** o ***Mere.*** (Rewi is the friend of Mary.)

In cases where the DEFINITE ARTICLE, *te*, forms part of a personal name (e.g. ***Te Maiharoa, Te Kooti***) this article belongs as part of the name in any construction.

e.g. *Ka* ***haere*** *a* ***Te Kooti.*** (Te Kooti goes.)
Ko ***Te Kooti*** *te* ***rangatira.*** (Te Kooti is the chief.)

LOCATION NOUNS

In Māori there is a small group of nouns which do not seem to have any parallel in English. These are words which refer to specific places or locations, in space or time, and are therefore called LOCATION NOUNS*.

Waho (the outside), ***runga*** (the top, the topside), ***uta*** (the shore, from seaward) are examples of this type of word.

Location nouns are not preceded by *he* or *te* or any other definitive, and they are the only type of base word† which can follow any of the LOCATION PREPOSITIONS (*ki, kei, i, hei*) directly (without any intervening word).

* In Williams' dictionary and other books these words are called LOCAL NOUNS. In *Let's Learn Maori* they are called LOCATIVES. However, the term LOCATION NOUN — it is used in Lyndsay Head's *Making Maori Sentences* — seems to me the clearest, and is therefore adopted here.)

† Except variant forms of the pronoun ***au***, such as ***ahau*** and ***awau***.

The reason these location nouns are difficult to relate to any English words is because they are not used in the same way as common nouns, but are used (quite logically) in the manner of place names.

To illustrate this —

in English we can say:	'at Oamaru'
and, similarly, in Māori:	*'kei **Oamaru**'*

In English, however, we have prepositions such as 'on', 'in', 'under', 'outside' for referring to the location of things. We can form such phrases as: 'on the table', 'outside the door'.

In English, this kind of statement is made in a single phrase. In Māori two phrases are required, with a base word in each, as in the following constructions:

*kei **runga***	*i te **tēpu,***	*kei **waho***	*i te **kūaha***
at topside	of the table	at outside	of the door

All place-names (e.g. ***Oamaru, Rotorua*** etc.) are classified as location nouns. Apart from the place-names, there seems to be less than 30 location nouns in the language which are at all commonly used — such as:

runga	the top side, the south
raro	the under side, the north
mua	the front
muri	the rear
roto	the inside
waho	the outside
waenga or ***waenganui***	the middle
tāwāhi or ***tarawāhi***	the other side (of sea, river or valley)
tua	the other side (of something solid — e.g. a hill)
tai	the sea, the shore from landward
uta	the inland, the shore from seaward
tahaki	one side, or the shore from seaward
hea? or ***whea?***	where?
konei	here
konā	there (near person spoken to)

korā	there (yonder)
reira	there (previously mentioned)
āianei	today
āpōpō	tomorrow
nanahi	yesterday
aoake	the day before or the day after
nehe or nehera	the ancient times

Several more location nouns may be found (classified l.n. for 'Local noun') in Williams' dictionary. Also see p. XXXIII of the introduction to that dictionary.

Further Reading

The three different types of NOUN described in this chapter are studied as three distinct classes of base words in *Let's Learn Maori* — that is, as 'NOUNS', 'PERSONALS' (a class which includes the personal pronouns) and 'LOCATIVES'.

CHAPTER 8

Verbs used as Nouns and Derived Nouns

The nouns of the three types considered in the previous chapter are all words which are not used as verbs. Most verbs, however, may be used as nouns.

All action verbs may be used as COMMON NOUNS, without any alteration whatsoever. For example, the action verb ***waiata*** (to sing) may be used in phrases such as *te* ***waiata*** (the song); ***kōrero*** (to speak) may be used as in ***tēnei kōrero*** (this speech) and ***mahi*** (to work) may be used as in *tāku* ***mahi*** (my work).

Most stative verbs may also be used as COMMON NOUNS, without alteration. For example ***pai*** (to be good) may be used as *te* ***pai*** (the goodness), ***ora*** (to be alive and healthy) may be used as in *te* ***ora*** (the life and/or well-being) and ***rangatira*** (to be esteemed) may be used as *te* ***rangatira*** (the esteemed person, the chief).

Some stative verbs, however, are most unlikely ever to be found used as nouns — or, at least, not other than in the form of DERIVED NOUNS as follows.

DERIVED NOUNS

The kinds of alterations which occur to base words in Māori are not nearly as great as those which occur in English.

One of the changes which does occur, however, is that of the addition of SUFFIXES, in the form of 'noun-endings', to verbs (action or stative) to create DERIVED NOUNS (called 'DERIVED' because they are derived from verbs).

The 'noun-ending' used may be any one of the following:

– nga	***– anga***		***– hanga***	***– kanga***
– manga	***– ranga***	***– tanga***	***– whanga***	***– inga***

Thus, from the action verb ***noho*** (to sit or stay) is derived the noun ***nohoanga*** (seat). From the action verb ***tangi*** (to cry out) is derived the noun ***tangihanga*** (the occasion of crying out — funeral). From the stative verb ***rangatira*** (to be esteemed or chiefly) is derived the noun ***rangatiratanga*** (chieftainship or sovereignty).

Which endings are used with which verbs is something to be learnt through practice. Another point to be noticed is that when a verb has a reduplicated first syllable, such as ***titiro*** (to see) and ***pupuri*** (to hold, to keep) the initial syllable is commonly dropped from the derived noun.

e.g. ***titiro*** (to see) → *te* ***tirohanga*** (the view).

The meaning of a derived noun is somewhat different to the meaning of just the unaltered verb used as a noun.

e.g. ***tangi*** (to cry) → *te* ***tangi*** (the cry)
→ *te* ***tanghihanga*** (the occasion of crying — the funeral)

e.g. ***rangatira*** (to be esteemed) → *te* ***rangatira*** (the esteemed person, the chief)
→ *te* ***rangatiratanga*** (the chieftainship or sovereignty)

Quite frequently (perhaps for variation) a construction using a derived noun will be preferred to the verb form.

e.g. The same sense as

Ka ***mea***	*a* ***Rewi***	*ki a*	***Mere,***
Said	Rewi	to	Mary,

might be rendered

Ko te ***meatanga***	*a* ***Rewi***	*ki a*	***Mere,***
The saying	of Rewi	to	Mary,

CHAPTER 9

Particles 1: In General, and the Particle *mā*

PARTICLES are, as has been noted, the lesser words which are associated with the base words to form phrases and connect phrases into sentences.

Confusion can arise in the learning of Māori if there is an assumption that an English meaning can be given to each word in Māori.

An English meaning can be given to base words.

e.g. ***aroha***	=	'to love', 'to show compassion towards' etc.
rākau	=	'tree', 'stick', 'something wooden' etc.

Particles, however, do not have any 'meaning' in the same sense at all. Particles supply certain kinds of secondary information about the base words.

For example, the DEFINITE ARTICLE, *te*, before a base word, supplies the information that the word is a NOUN (or another type of base word being used as a noun) in the singular.

e.g. *Ko **tēnei***	*te **waiata**.*	
this	the song	(This is the song.)

The DEFINITE ARTICLE, *ngā*, before a base word supplies the information that the base word is functioning as a NOUN in the plural.

e.g. *Ko **ēnei***	*ngā*	***waiata.***	
these	the	songs	(These are the songs.)

The VERBAL PARTICLE, *i*, establishes that the action (of the verb following) took place in the past.

I ***waiata***	***rātou.***	
sang	they	(They sang.)

Sometimes particles can be translated by English words, but they do not have fixed English equivalents, and may correspond to different English words in different contexts.

For example the particle *'ki'* may often be appropriately translated by the English 'to', as in:

ki te ***toa*** (to the shop)

but in other contexts *ki* may have closer correspondence with 'at', 'by', 'for', 'against', 'according to' or some other word or words. In some contexts it will be an extra word in the Māori phrase, requiring no equivalent at all in English, as in:

Ka ***aroha***	***au***	*ki a* ***koe.***	
love	I	you	(I love you.)

Particles have a grammatical function that is quite logical in Māori but which will not necessarily translate into English. This means we simply have to learn the function and significance of each of the particles in the Māori context.

There are only about 60 particles, and the structure of Māori becomes much clearer if one is able to distinguish base words from particles easily, and thus perceive the patterns of phrases.

It needs to be noted that the sound (and spelling — sometimes just a single letter) of some particles is identical to that of others with quite different functions. In such cases the particles concerned must be regarded as quite separate and distinct words, one from the other.

For example, the particle *me* functions as at least three separate words:

(i) a PREPOSITION (with uses similar to 'if' and 'like')

e.g.	*Me he* ***manu***	***ahau*** *. . .*	
	If a bird	I	(If I were a bird . . .)

(ii) a VERBAL PARTICLE (used to indicate that the action of a verb ought to be done')

e.g.	*Me* ***haere***	***au.***	
	Ought to go	I	(I ought to go.)

(iii) another PREPOSITION (with uses similar to certain uses of 'with' and 'and')

e.g. *te **rangi*** *me te **whenua***
the heaven and the earth

Similarly, ***kei*** has uses which include that of a PREPOSITION ('at' in the present tense).

e.g. *Kei te **kūaha*** (At the door)

as well as that of a VERBAL PARTICLE (signifying a warning against the occurrence of the action or state referred to by the verb).

e.g. *Kei **hinga*** ***koe.***
Don't become fallen you (Don't you fall.)

It could be noted here that whereas the simplest translation, 'fall', is an English verb of action, the Māori word ***hinga*** is a stative verb. Commands or instructions 'not to do something', using action verbs (and only action verbs) in Māori are commonly expressed using the negative formula ***Kaua*** *e* . . . referred to on p. 107.

The particles *a*, *e* and *i* each have several distinct uses, which means that each must be considered to represent several quite different words.

For instance, the particle *a* is quite a different word in each of the following cases:

(a) *te **tama*** *a **Hata*** (the son of Hata)
here *a* = 'of' (where possessor is 'superior').

(b) *E **haere** ana* *a **Hata*** (Hata is going)
here *a* = untranslateable 'personal article' marking the unemphasized subject of the sentence.

(c) *Ka **haere** mai* ***rātou*** *a te **Mane.***
(They will come on Monday.)
here *a* is used for referring to future time.

Different uses of *e* and *i* are considered at other places in this book. The point to be made here is simply that, with these identical particles, initially at least, care needs to be taken to distinguish which one is being used in a given context.

* * * *

Particles may be separated, in the first instance, into two broad categories:

(a) particles which precede the base word or words in a phrase
(b) particles which follow the base word or words in a phrase.

Certain particles which usually follow base words (e.g. *nei*) may, on occasions, be placed before the base, but it would seem that only one particle (*anō*) is used with roughly equal frequency in either position.

Within each broad category further grouping of the particles is possible, as follows:

Checklist of Particles

PARTICLES WHICH PRECEDE BASES

Articles
te ngā he a

Prepositions
ko me (and) *me* (if) *a* (of) *o nā nō mā*
mō i e (by) *a* (future time) *e* (address)

Location Prepositions
ki kei (or *kai*) *i hei* (or *hai*)

Possesive Particles
tā tō ā ō

Verbal Particles
ka e kua i me kia kei (or *kai*) *ina*

Adverbial Particle
*anō**

PARTICLES WHICH FOLLOWS BASES

Position Particles
nei na ra

* Also using after bases.

DIRECTION PARTICLES (ADVERBIAL)

mai *atu* *ake* *iho*

OTHER ADVERBIAL PARTICLES

ai *anake* *anō** *hoki* *kau* *kē* *koa* *noa* *pea* *rawa* *tonu*

VERBAL PARTICLE

ana

UNCLASSIFIED PARTICLE

mā (see below)

A complete study of all the uses of all the particles is beyond the scope of this book. What is attempted here is simply a guide, in brief, to the primary significance of each of these particles (counting *anō* only once, the total is 53), and referral to other, more detailed and authoritative sources, for further information. (See Note 1, p. 118.)

The next four chapters cover those particles which are used exclusively or most commonly with words functioning as nouns. The other groups are returned to at Chapter 20, after the chapters on verbs.

The unclassified particle *mā* is, however, covered separately here:

THE PARTICLE *MĀ*

This word, quite distinct from the preposition *mā* (for) and the stative verb ***mā*** (to be white or clean) is placed after people's names to give the sense of 'and accompanying others'.

e.g. *Ko **Māui** mā* — Māui and others accompanying him.

Placed after terms of address, such as ***hoa*** (friend) or ***tamariki*** (children) or after the pronouns ***wai*** or ***mea***, it simply emphasizes that more than one person is being referred to.

e.g. *Tēnā **koutou***	*e **hoa** mā!*	(Greetings, friends!)
*Ko **wai** mā*	***ēnei**?*	(Who are these?)

Perhaps it is the same word as that used in counting above ten.

e.g. ***Tekau** mā **tahi*** — (ten and one, eleven)

* Also used preceding bases.

CHAPTER 10

Particles 2: Articles

te *ngā* *he* *a*

All articles directly precede the first base word in any phrase in which they occur.

DEFINITE ARTICLES : *TE* AND *NGĀ*

te (singular) and *ngā* (plural) mark the base word following as a NOUN (or verb functioning as a noun) singular and plural respectively.

e.g. *te* ***manu***	the bird	*ngā* ***manu***	the birds
te ***waiata***	the song	*ngā* ***waiata***	the songs

INDEFINITE ARTICLE : *HE*

Preceding a NOUN (or an ACTION VERB, which, with *he*, functions as a noun) *he* does not specify number.

e.g. *he* ***manu*** can mean 'a bird' 'some birds' or just 'birds'
he ***waiata*** can mean 'a song' 'some songs' or just 'songs'

With a STATIVE VERB, *he* gives the sense of a descriptive, verbal phrase.

e.g. *He* ***whero***	*te* ***whare.***	
Is red	the house	(The house is red.)

he is also used in asking the question *He* ***aha*** . . . ? ('What?' or 'What is ?') and the whole phrase, *He* ***aha***, is used, with *ai* following the verb, in asking 'why?'

e.g. *He* ***aha*** ***koe*** *i* ***haere*** *ai?* (Why did you go?)

he is also used in a particular construction with ***mea*** (thing) which introduces a verb.

e.g. *He* ***mea hanga***	*na te* ***Atua***
created	God

i te ***timatanga***	*te* ***rangi***	*me te* ***whenua.***
in the beginning	the heaven	and the earth

In the beginning God created the heaven and the earth

A further use is in *Me he* ***mea*** (or *Mehe****mea***) . . . (If . . .).

he is usually the first word in any phrase in which it occurs; and it is not used after a preposition (except, on occasions, *me*) — either the definite article, *te*, is substituted or some other word, such as ***tētahi*** (a certain) or ***ētahi*** (some) is used.

e.g.	*te* ***utu***	*mo te* ***tīketi***	
	the price	for the ticket	(the price of a ticket)

PERSONAL ARTICLE : *A*

This article really has no counterpart in English. It stands immediately before PERSONAL NOUNS, PERSONAL PRONOUNS and LOCATION NOUNS in the following situations:

(1) before PERSONAL NOUNS and LOCATION NOUNS when they are the unemphasized SUBJECT of a sentence.

e.g.	*Ka* ***haere***	*a* ***Mere.***	(Mary goes.)
	Ka ***wera***	*a* ***waho.***	(The outside is burnt.)
	He ***tāone***	*a* ***Oamaru.***	(Oamaru is a town.)

(When the subject is emphasised it may be placed at the beginning of the sentence, and introduced by the preposition *ko*, or in another type of construction, by *nā* or *mā*. See under *ko*, *nā* and *mā*.)

(2) before all PERSONAL NOUNS and PERSONAL PRONOUNS (except variants of ***au***, such as ***ahau***) after any of the LOCATION PREPOSITIONS *ki*, *kei*, *i* or *hei*.

e.g.	***Kōrero*** *atu*	*ki a* ***Mere.***	(Speak to Mary.)
	Kōrero *mai*	*ki a* ***au.***	(Speak to me.)
but	***Kōrero*** *mai*	*ki* ***ahau.***	(Speak to me.)

CHAPTER 11

Particles 3: Prepositions

As the name 'pre-position' indicates, any preposition is always the first word in any phrase in which it occurs. (Obviously, then, there can be only one preposition in any one phrase.)

The four LOCATION PREPOSITIONS are considered in Chapter 12, and different functions of *i* and *e* are studied in Chapter 24. The prepositions considered here are *ko* *me* *a* *o* *nā* *nō* *mā* *mō*

KO

ko (like the personal article, *a*) has no counterpart in English, and it is not necessarily easy to explain, in English, the significance of such a word. The use of such a word is better understood simply through practice. It could be said, though, that *ko* is called the 'focus preposition' because whatever base word it precedes is the focus of attention in the sentence.

ko commonly directly precedes either a PERSONAL PRONOUN, a PERSONAL NOUN or a LOCATION NOUN (and, rarely, a STATIVE VERB).

e.g.	*Ko* ***rātou***	*ngā* ***tāngata.***	
	They	the people	(They are the people.)
	Ko ***Hōri***	*tōku* ***papa.***	
	George	my father	(George is my father.)
	Ko ***Otepoti***	*te* ***tāone.***	
	Dunedin	the town	(Dunedin is the town.)

When the word in focus is a COMMON NOUN, some form of DEFINITIVE* will stand between *ko* and the noun.

e.g.	*Ko te* ***maunga***	***tēnei.***	
	the mountain	this	(This is the mountain.)

* See Chap. 15.

Some definitives (such as ***tēnei***) also, when standing alone in a phrase, may be the focus, and are then directly preceded by *ko*.

e.g.	*Ko* ***tēnei***	*te* ***maunga.***	
	This	the mountain	(This is the mountain.)

ME

me will frequently be translated by 'and', but 'and' will only in some contexts be appropriately translated by *me* — usually where the 'and' has the sense of 'together with'.

e.g.	*te* ***rangi***	*me te* ***whenua***
	the heaven	and the earth

me can also have the sense of 'if', and also has a function as a verbal particle (see pp. 42 and 76).

A AND *O*

Both *a* and *o* commonly correspond to 'of' (in the sense of 'belonging to'). Which one is used depends upon the type of relationship between the possessor and the thing possessed. This is quite a complicated feature of Māori, and several books deal with it in various manners.* Briefly, it might be said that where the possessor is superior to the thing possessed *a* is used.

e.g.	*Ko te*	***pukapuka***	*a* ***Rewi***	
	the	book	of Rewi	(Rewi's book)

But where the thing possessed is superior, *o* is used.

Ko te	***whaea***	*o* ***Rewi***	
the	mother	of Rewi	(Rewi's mother)

One way of remembering this is: ***o* for things that are 'over'.**

As well as things that are obviously 'superior', however, the *o* category also includes personal names, parts of things, qualities of things, feelings, clothing, water, medicine, houses, means of transport, and

* See the 'Further Reading' section at the end of this chapter.

actions (in relation to the receiver). (Actions, in relation to the 'doer', are governed by *a*.)

NĀ AND NŌ

Both *nā* and *nō* signify 'belonging to', by right of ownership established in the past, and the same distinction of *a* and *o* categories applies.

e.g. *Nā* ***Rewi***	*tēnei* ***pene.***	
Belonging to Rewi	this pen	(This pen is Rewi's.)
Nō ***Rewi***	*tēnei* ***whare.***	
Belonging to Rewi	this house	(This house is Rewi's.)

The question *Nō* ***hea koe***? is commonly taken to be asking 'Where are you from?' In a sense, it really asks 'Where do you belong?' or 'Where is your place of origin?'

nā is also used in a particular type of construction to give emphasis to who DID something.

e.g. *Nā* ***Rewi***	*i* ***mau***	*ngā* ***ika.****
Rewi	brought	the fish.

MĀ AND MŌ

The *a* and *o* distinction also applies with *mā* and *mō*, both of which also signify 'belonging to' — but in this case the ownership is to be established in the future.

e.g. *Mā* ***Mere***	*ēnei* ***ika.***	
For Mary	these fish	(These fish are for Mary.)
Mō ***Rewi***	*tēnei* ***whare.***	
For Rewi	this house.	(This house is for Rewi.)

mā is also used (in a construction similar to *nā*, above) to give emphasis to who will do something.

e.g. *Mā* ***Rewi***	*e* ***mau***	*ngā* ***ika.****
Rewi	will bring	the fish.

* See Chap. 26, Emphasis on the actor.

mō is widely used in various situations where it will translate as 'for' or 'of'

e.g. *He **aha***	*te **utu***	*mō te **tīketi**?*
What	the price	for the ticket?

In English it would be more usual to ask the price for (or of) a ticket, but it should be remembered that the Māori indefinite article (*he* — 'a' or 'some') is not used after prepositions.

Another very common use of *mō* corresponds to 'about' (in the sense of 'concerning').

e.g. *He **kōrero***	*mō **Mere**.*
A story	about (or concerning) Mary.

As with other Māori prepositions, *mō* has no fixed counterpart in English. It will be translated by different English words according to context. Similarly, an English preposition such as 'for' will only in some contexts be appropriately translated by *mō*. In other contexts different Māori words (such as *hai* or *hei*) will be required.

These last four POSSESIVE PREPOSITIONS (*nā*, *nō*, *mā* and *mō*) are also very important in that, in combination with the PERSONAL PRONOUNS, they form widely used sets of POSSESSIVES (see Chap. 25).

Further Reading

In many, if not all, languages, the correct use of the prepositions is one of the more difficult things to learn. There are at least two reasons for this. Regarding the differences between English and Māori, it can be said that:

(a) In Māori prepositions are used in situations where English doesn't require them (see particularly Chap. 24).

(b) No prepositions in one of the languages have exact counterparts in the other language. (That is, different words will be required for translation in different contexts.)

However, this does not need to impair one's understanding of Māori. Since the main meaning of any sentence is conveyed in the base words, if one focuses on that meaning (i.e. the meaning of the base words) the function of the preposition used will, in most cases, be fairly obvious — and familiarity with the prepositions may thus be acquired. (This is just one way of saying that practice is the best teacher.)

The entries for each of the prepositions in Williams' dictionary provide carefully chosen examples of use. For translating from English into Māori, on the other hand, the entries for English prepositions ('at', 'by', 'for', 'with' etc.) may be consulted in the *English-Maori Dictionary* by H.M. Ngata in order to choose, from the range offered, the correct word for the context. (In some cases care needs to be taken, however, in understanding exactly which of the words in a given phrase is the preposition.)

Further information on the *a* and *o* categories of possession is provided by Professor Patu Hohepa in Appendix 1 of the above-mentioned H.M. Ngata dictionary. This aspect of Māori is also covered in Section 13 of *Let's Learn Maori* (in which book, also, the use of prepositions is given much coverage in several sections).

CHAPTER 12

Particles 4: Location Prepositions

ki *kei* (or *kai*) *i* *hei* (or *hai*)

These four prepositions are treated as a group because they all have a common characteristic. LOCATION NOUNS are the only* BASE WORDS which they directly precede. All four refer to location in some way.

ki refers either to actual movement or to some mental or emotional transference from one location to another.

e.g. ***Haere** mai*	*ki **konei**.*	
Come	to this place.	(Come here.)
Titiro	*ki te **pukapuka**.*	
Look	at the book.	

kei, i and *hei* could all be said to have some correspondence to the English preposition 'at' (or, variously 'on' or 'in') with the distinction that each carries additional information as follows:

kei = 'at' in the present tense
i = 'at' in the past tense
hei = 'at' in the future tense

e.g. *Kei te **whare***	***ia**.*	
is at the house	she	(She **is** at the house.)
*I te **whare***	***au**.*	
was at the house	I	(I **was** at the house.)
*Hei te **whare***	***ia**.*	
will be at the house	he	(He **will** be at the house.)
*I te **tīmatanga***	*te **kupu**.*	
Was at the beginning	the word	(In the beginning **was** the word.)

* The exceptions — ***'ahau'*** etc — have previously been noted.

Although *kei te...* and *i te...* are not intrinsically verbal constructions, some dialects use these constructions with verbs (both action and stative).

e.g. *Kei te **mahi***	***ia.***	
is at the work	she	(She **is** working.)
*I te **mahi***	***ia.***	
was at the work	he	(He **was** working.)

These constructions generally, in Eastern dialects, replace the Northern and Western construction using *e ... ana* (for which see Chap. 20, VERBAL PARTICLES).

(Note: *hei* does not seem to be used in this manner, but *Kei te...* is used for the future, just as in English we might say 'She is working tomorrow.')

The *kei te...* construction is widely heard in the common exchange of greetings:

*Kei te **pēhea***	***koe?***	(How are you?)
*Kei te **pai***	***au.***	(I'm fine.)

Just as there is no equivalent of the verb 'to be' in Māori, so, also is there no verb in Māori corresponding to the English verb 'to have' (in the sense of 'possessing'). *Kei, i* and *hei* are also used in one way of expressing the sense of having.

e.g. *Kei a **Mere***	*te **pene**.*	
Is at Mary	the pen	(Mary has the pen.)
I** a **koe	*te **pene**.*	
Was at you	the pen	(You had the pen.)

Again, it should be noted that the untranslatable PERSONAL ARTICLE, *a*, comes between any of these four LOCATION PREPOSITIONS and any PERSONAL NOUN or PRONOUN, except ***'ahau'*** etc.

Note could also be made here that almost any statement in Māori can be made into a question simply by intonation in speech or a question-mark in writing.

e.g.	*Kei a* ***Mere***	*te* ***pene****?*	
	Is at Mary	the pen?	(Does Mary have the pen?)

hei is commonly used with the sense of 'for', meaning 'for the purpose of'.

e.g.	*Ko ēnei* ***ika***	*hei* ***kai***	*mā* ***kōrua****.*
	These fish (are)	for food	for you two.

Further Reading

Suggestions for further reading about prepositions are given in the previous chapter. What could be emphasized here is that the words *i* and *kei*, as LOCATION PREPOSITIONS, need to be clearly distinguished from the words *i* and *kei* as VERBAL PARTICLES.

The use of *i* as a LOCATION PREPOSITION should also be distinguished from its other, different prepositional uses (e.g. see p. 89) all of which should, ideally, be clearly distinguished, one from the other. (Williams' dictionary lists 18 separate uses of *i* as a preposition.) *ki* has almost as many different prepositional uses (16 in Williams' dictionary).

The different uses of *i* and *ki* probably represent the most complicated of all the uses of prepositions in Māori. They are studied in considerable detail in *Let's Learn Maori* (particularly in Sections 6 and 32).

CHAPTER 13

Particles 5: The Possessive Particles

tā, tō, ā, ō

The particles *tā* and *tō* are considered to be contractions of *te... a* ('the... of') and *te... o* (also 'the... of') respectively.

Thus

te pukapuka	***a Rewi***	
the book	of Rewi	(Rewi's book)

may equally be expressed in the form

tā Rewi pukapuka (Rewi's book)

and

te whaea	***o Rewi***	
the mother	of Rewi	(Rewi's mother)

may equally be expressed in the form

tō Rewi whaea (Rewi's mother)

ā and *ō* are the plural forms.

Thus:

ā Rewi pukapuka (Rewi's books)

and

ō Rewi mātua (Rewi's parents)

These types of constructions are probably not as commonly used as the constructions using *te... a* and *te... o* (or, in the plural, *ngā... a* and *ngā... o*) but these four POSSESSIVE PARTICLES (*tā, tō, ā* and *ō*) along with *nā, nō, mā* and *mō*, are very important in forming, in combination with the PERSONAL PRONOUNS, sets of POSSESSIVES which are very basic to Māori (see Chap. 25).

CHAPTER 14

Particles 6: The Position Particles

nei na ra

Any of these particles usually stands after (not necessarily directly after) the last base word in any phrase in which it occurs. Like all particles which follow bases these may be said to be adverbial in nature — adding some qualification to the base word or words.

nei signifies 'position here, near the person speaking'.

e.g. *te* ***tamaiti*** *nei* 'the child here'

na signifies 'position there, near the person spoken to'.

e.g. *te* ***kūaha*** *na* 'the door there, by you'.

ra signifies 'position there, separate from both speaker and person spoken to'.

e.g. *ngā* ***manu*** *ra* 'the birds yonder'.

In all of the above examples the base words are nouns. The position particles may, however, also occur with verbs.

e.g. *te* ***whare***	*e* ***tū*** *nei*
the house	standing here

In such cases, the position particle may be considered to be substituting for the verbal particle *una* (see further on p. 76).

Whilst these particles usually follow base words, *nei*, at least, is sometimes found preceding the base.*

e.g. ***tāku***	*nei*	***mahi***	
my	here	work	(my work here)

* See *Let's Learn Maori*, p. 49.

These three position particles are also very important in forming various compound words, such as the set of DEFINITIVES, ***tēnei, tēnā*** etc. (see next chapter) as well as the LOCATION NOUNS ***konei, konā, korā*** and the ACTION VERBS ***pēnei, pēnā, pērā*** as follows:

Compounds are formed with the location noun base ***kō*** (yonder place) to produce the following set of LOCATION NOUNS (note should be taken of the changes in vowel-length):

konei	this place here
konā	that place there (near person spoken to)
korā	that place there (yonder)

e.g. *Kei* ***konei*** ***au.*** (I am here.)

A word for 'Here is...' or 'Here are...' is ***anei.***

e.g. ***Anei*** *ōu* ***hū.*** (Here are your shoes.)

Compounds are also formed with the base ***pē*** to create a set of ACTION VERBS:

pēnei (-tia)*	do like this	
pēnā (-tia)	do like that	(associated with person spoken to)
pērā (-tia)	do like that	(associated with somewhere else)

e.g. *kia* ***pēnei*** *tā* ***koutou inoi*** (do your prayer like this)

Like most other BASE WORDS, these words can also be used descriptively.

e.g. ***Hōmai*** *he* ***pene pēnei.*** (Give me a pen like this.)

Note: The base of these words, ***pē***, is apparently not found other than in these compounds and in ***pēhea***† (***-tia***) — an interrogative ACTION VERB with a meaning something like 'do, in what way?' or 'how?' — widely used in greetings:

e.g. *E* ***pēhea*** *ana* ***koe***? (How are you?)

In northern dialects, however, one hears this word (***pēhea***) reduced almost to simply the base ***pē***:

e.g. ***Pē*** *ana* ***koe***? (How are you?)

* The suffix, in brackets, is the 'passive ending' for the verb. See further on pp. 65-66.
\+ Dialect variant *pēwhea* (*-tia*).

CHAPTER 15

Definitives

The grouping of words which may be called DEFINITIVES is comprised of

(a) the DEFINITE ARTICLES *te* and *ngā* (see Chap. 10)
(b) the POSSESSIVE PARTICLES *tā, tō, ā* and *ō* (see Chap. 13) and the POSSESSIVES formed from them (see Chap. 25)
(c) the words considered in this chapter.

All definitives have singular and plural forms, the plural being made in all cases except that of *te* (plural — *ngā*) simply by dropping the initial *t** from the singular.

One set of definitives is formed by combining the DEFINITE ARTICLE, *te*, with the different POSITION PARTICLES, *nei*, *na* and *ra*, as follows (the lengthening of all the single vowels should be noted):

SINGULAR		PLURAL	
tēnei	this	***ēnei***	these
tēnā	that (near listener)	***ēnā***	those (near listener)
tērā	that (yonder)	***ērā***	those (yonder)

There is not very much difference in English between the phrases 'the house here' and 'this house'. Neither is there in Māori any significant difference between —

	te ***whare*** *nei*	and	***tēnei whare***
or	*te* ***rākau*** *na*	and	***tēnā rākau***
or	*ngā* ***manu*** *ra*	and	***ērā manu*** etc.

Other important definitives are:

SINGULAR	PLURAL
tētahi a, one	***ētahi*** some
taua that (mentioned before)	***aua*** those (mentioned before)
tēhea†...? which...?	***ēhea***†...? which...?

* Some dialect forms replace the *t* with *w* (e.g. *wēnei* — 'these').
† Or *tēwhea* and *ēwhea*.

The definitive ***taua*** (that, mentioned before) always needs to be clearly distinguished from the personal pronoun ***tāua*** ('you and I').

As well as being used before words functioning as nouns, the definitives referred to in this chapter may also be used as pronouns — that is, as words standing in place of nouns. In this function they may stand as sole base words in phrases (just as their normal English translations are used). (This is the reason these words are shown in bold print in this book.)

e.g. *Ko* ***tēnei*** *te* ***whare.*** (This is the house.)
Hōmai ētahi. (Give me one.)

As well as standing as impersonal pronouns in this manner, ***tēnei, tēnā, tērā*** and ***ēnei, ēnā, ērā*** may also be used for referring to people.

e.g. *Ko* ***wai tērā****?*
(Who (is) that (person) over there?)

Tēnei, tēnā and ***tērā*** can also be used as base words with the sense of 'here', 'there' (near listener) and 'there' (yonder) respectively.

e.g. ***Tēnei*** *tonu* ***mātou.*** (Here we are.)

One of the most common uses of ***tēnā*** in this sense is in the standard greetings ***Tēnā koe!, Tēnā kōrua!*** and ***Tēnā koutou!*** where it seems to serve the purpose of a formal acknowledgement of the presence of the person or people being greeted.

CHAPTER 16

Base Words 3: Verbs in General

All verbs in Māori (that is, both action verbs and stative verbs) are really much simpler than verbs in English. Verbs in English undergo several different alterations, depending on who (or what) is doing an action and on when it is being done.

For example, with the English verb 'to go', we say 'I go.' but 'She goes.' In the past tense it is 'She went.' In the future 'She will go.' and in the past perfect tense 'She has gone.' There are a great number of such different, irregular, changes in verbs in English which present difficulties in learning.

In Māori, although verbs may be given passive endings (see below) there is nothing like the range of irregularities that occur in English.

Verbs, in Māori, are marked as verbs (except in some cases noted below) by the VERBAL PARTICLES used in association with them.

These particles supply different kinds of secondary information about the verb, but they do not, generally, create parallels to the tenses of English (an exception is the particle *i* which indicates simple past tense). The verbal constructions of Māori, rather, cut obliquely across the tenses of English.

The particle *ka*, for instance, is used to indicate that an action (or state of being) is recognised as beginning at the point of time established by the context (i.e. it may be in the past, present or future).

Thus, if a simple statement such as —

*Ka **haere***	*a **Mere**.*
goes	Mary

is considered on its own, it may appear that any of several translations of meaning are possible — including 'Mary went.' 'Mary is going.' and 'Mary will go.'

At first, this may seem unsettling to anyone who is accustomed to a definite time-reference being an integral feature of a verb (as in English). It may even be something of a surprise to discover that specific 'time-marking' of the verb itself is not, after all, something that is absolutely essential to clear and precise communication.

This does not mean there will be any confusion in Māori about when something occurs. Time-marking of the verb itself (no matter how much we are used to it in English) is not essential because, in practice (in conversation or in writing) statements such as: *Ka **haere** a **Mere*** are simply never (except perhaps in grammar books!) made in isolation.

The context always provides enough information, in terms of a time-frame, to avoid any real confusion. (Even in English, in a statement such as 'I go to the shop yesterday.' whilst the form of the verb may be wrong, the meaning is quite clear.)

The following examples of verbs with *ka* should give some idea of its range of uses (the translations given are not necessarily the only ones possible):

Action Verbs with *ka*

*Ka **haere***	***tātou!***		
(Begin to) go	we	(Let's go!)	
*Ka **whakakitea** mai*	*e **ia***	*ki **ahau...***	
was shown	by him	to me (He showed me...)	
Katahi	*ka **waiata***	*a **Mohi***	***rātou***
Then	sang	Moses (and)	
*ko ngā **tama***	*a **Iharaira**.*		
the children	of Israel.		

(Moses and the children of Israel began to sing.)

STATIVE VERBS WITH *KA*

*Ka **pai***	***tēnā!***		
Is good	that	(That's good!)	
Na	*ka **oti***	*te **rangi***	*me te **whenua**.*
Then	were completed	the heavens	and the earth
*Ka **mate!***	*Ka **mate!***	*Ka **ora!***	*Ka **ora!***
Dead!	Dead!	Alive!	Alive!

With verbs in English (and many other languages) there are hundreds of variations and irregularities to be learnt. In Māori there are no changes in base words for tense-marking, and virtually no irregularities. The main things to be learnt in relation to verbs in Māori are:

(1) the significance of each of the VERBAL PARTICLES (and other particles which commonly follow verbs)

(2) the PASSIVE FORMS of action verbs (pp.65-66)

(3) the correct PREPOSITION (*i, ki* or *e*) to use for connecting an object with the verb (Chap. 24)

(4) the noun-ending each verb takes to form a DERIVED NOUN (Chap. 8).

CHAPTER 17

Base Words 4: Action Verbs

Words such as ***mahi*** (work), ***noho*** (sit, stay), ***aroha*** (love), ***waiata*** (sing) are ACTION VERBS. They refer to actions or things that can be done.

Action verbs are commonly (although not always) marked as verbs by the VERBAL PARTICLES used in conjunction with them.

These particles (*ka, kua, kia, kei* etc.) signify various different modes, aspects or conditions of the action (or, with stative verbs, the state) expressed by the verb. They do not, except in the case of *i* (which signifies simple past tense) act as counterparts to English tenses. The establishment of a time-sense in relation to a verb is generally supplied by the context.

The individual significance of each of the verbal particles is covered in Chapter 19. Here it might be emphasized again that verbs in Māori are much simpler than verbs in English (or those in many other languages) — provided that their essential simplicity is accepted, and there is no unreasonable reaching after exact correspondences with English that simply don't (and don't need to) exist.

Verbs in English go through many different changes (e.g. 'go', 'goes', 'going', 'gone', 'went' and 'sing', 'sings', 'singing', 'sung', 'sang').

Verbs in Māori may carry the prefix ***whaka-***; they may also be given passive endings (referred to below) but they do not (that is, the base words themselves do not) go through changes like those of English verbs.

e.g. *Ka* ***haere*** ***rātou.***
go they
('They went.' 'They are going.' or 'They will go.')

E ***haere*** *ana* ***rātou.***
going they
('They were going.' 'They are going.' or 'They will be going.')

Kua ***haere***	***rātou.***
gone	they

('They had gone.' 'They have gone.' or 'They will have gone.')

I ***haere***	***rātou.***
went	they (They went.)

It can be seen that the base word, ***haere***, remains constant throughout.

There are hundreds of verb variations in English. In Māori there are scarcely more than a dozen constructions, with different particles, to learn. These constructions may then be used with any verb.

Further information is given in Chapter 19 (on verbal particles). A scheme of the Māori verb is given on page xxxviii of Williams' dictionary.

THE PREFIX *WHAKA-*

Action verbs may be prefixed by the 'causative' prefix ***whaka-***.

e.g. ***haere***	means	'to move or to go'
whakahaere	means	'to cause to go' — 'to organise'
rongo	means	'to hear'
whakarongo	means	'to cause to hear' — 'to listen'
ako	means	'to learn'
whakaako	means	'to cause to learn' — 'to teach'

ACTIVE AND PASSIVE

The distinguishing characteristic of ACTION VERBS, as a class of base words, is that they can be used in either an ACTIVE or a PASSIVE form. In the passive form, one of a range of PASSIVE ENDINGS is given to the verb.

The active form is used when someone (or something) is DOING the action.

e.g. *Ka* ***aroha*** *te* ***kōtiro.*** (The girl loves.)

The passive form is used when the action is DONE TO someone (or something).

e.g. *Ka* ***arohaina*** *te* ***kōtiro.*** (The girl is loved.)

Passive endings always terminate in ***-a***, but they may (according to Williams' dictionary) be any of the following forms: ***-a, -hia, -kia, -mia, -ngia, -ria, -tia, -whia, -na, -ina, -hina, -kina, -rina, -whina, -nga, -hanga.***

Although some action verbs may have more than one alternative passive ending, for most action verbs one of the above forms will be the regular, usual form — but it seems that no comprehensive rules can be established to predetermine which ending is correct for any particular verb.

With regard to understanding Māori it can become relatively easy to identify verbs as being used in the passive sense. In learning a vocabulary of action verbs however, the attempt should be made to learn the correct passive ending for each.

The passive forms of action verbs are commonly shown in dictionaries and glossaries in some such manner as the following (and henceforward will be shown thus in this book):

aroha (***-ina***)
titiro (***tirohia***)*

Not infrequently an action verb may both carry the prefix whaka- and be in the passive form.

e.g. ***whakakitea*** (shown)

Here the action verb is ***kite*** (***-a***) — 'to see'. Thus, ***whakakitea*** means 'to be caused to be seen' (i.e. to be 'shown' or 'exhibited').

Another base word, or an adverbial particle, 'modifying' a passive verb may be given an ending (usually ***tia***) in 'agreement' with the verb.

e.g. ***I kainga katoatia ngā kai.*** (The food was completely eaten.)
(See Williams' dictionary, introduction, p. XXXVI.)

* As with derived nouns, reduplicated first syllables are commonly dropped. In such cases, the passive form of the verb is often (as here) given in full.

COMMANDS

Commands, instructions or invitations to do something can be given in different ways in Māori.

The action verb may be simply used on its own.

e.g. ***Haere!*** (Go!)
Titiro! (Look!)

Sometimes it will carry the prefix whaka-

e.g. ***Whakarongo!*** (Listen!)

Sometimes it will be followed by a direction particle.

e.g. ***Haere*** *mai!* (Come here!)
Haere *atu!* (Go away!)
Whakarongo *mai!* (Listen!)

Where the verb has no more than two short vowels (or one long vowel) it will be preceded by the particle *e*.

e.g. *E* ***tū!*** (Stand up!)
E ***kai!*** (Eat up!)

The *e* will not be used, however, if the verb is followed by another particle.

e.g. ***Tū*** *mai!* (Stand up!)

Another way of giving a command is by using the PASSIVE form of an action verb. e.g. With ***tō*** (***-ia***) — 'to pull':

Tōia *mai* ***te waka!*** (Pull hither the canoe!)

In this form of command, some object is always the passive receiver of the action. In the above example it is 'the canoe', and the sentence could be translated as 'Let the canoe be pulled hither'. Even where the object is not stated, however, it will still at least be implied e.g. ***Nohoia!*** (Sit down!) implies some seat being sat upon. (This command or invitation could, in fact, be worded ***Nohoia*** *te* ***tūru!*** — Let the chair be sat upon!)

Action Verbs used as Nouns

As explained in Chapter 8, Māori action verbs may also be used as nouns.

e.g. ***mahi*** (-***a***) 'to work'; *te* ***mahi*** 'the work'
waiata (-***tia***) 'to sing'; *te* ***waiata*** 'the song'
kai (-***nga***) 'to eat'; *te* ***kai*** 'the food'

To form some kinds of noun, however, the verb will be given one of a range of noun-endings.

e.g. ***noho*** (-***ia***) 'to sit'; *te* ***nohoanga*** 'the seat'
mahi (-***a***) 'to work'; *te* ***mahinga*** 'the cultivation'

Action Verbs used as Adjectives

Action verbs can also be used to add description to nouns. When used in this manner the verb will normally follow the noun.

e.g. ***kai*** (-***nga***)	is an action verb meaning 'to eat'
te ***whare kai***	means 'the eating house' or 'dining hall'.
noho (-***ia***)	is an action verb meaning 'to sit or stay'
te ***whare noho***	thus means 'the staying house' or 'accommodation'.

Further Reading

The term 'action verb' replaces, in this book, the term 'universal' used in *Let's Learn Maori*. Authority (if not necessarily approval) for this change is taken from page 31 of that book — 'universals express actions.'

Thus, any section concerned with 'universals' in *Let's Learn Maori* will concern the type of word called, in this book, 'action verb'.

In Williams' dictionary none of the terms 'universal', 'stative' or 'stative verb' are used. 'Verbs' are simply distinguished as 'transitive' (v.t.) and 'intransitive' (v.i.). Many stative verbs are classified as 'adjectives' (a.).

CHAPTER 18

Base Words 5: Stative Verbs

Words such as ***tūpato*** (to be careful), ***ora*** (to be alive and well), ***pai*** (to be good or fine), ***mutu*** (to be finished — in the sense of 'ceased'), ***mahue*** (to be left behind) and ***rangatira*** (to be esteemed) are considered to be STATIVE VERBS. They express, or refer to, the 'state of being' of someone or something.

What distinguishes stative verbs most significantly from action verbs is that stative verbs do not, normally, take passive endings* (their meaning is always, in a sense, 'passive').

All stative verbs may be used with the same particles as action verbs, although the range of constructions commonly encountered is not as great as that of action verbs.

Here are some examples of simple sentences with stative verbs used with verbal particles —

*Ka **pai***	***tēnā!***	
is good	that	(That's good!)
*Ka **ora***	*te **tamaiti**.*	
is alive and well	the child	(The child is alive and well.)
*Kia **ora***	e ***koe***!	
be alive and well	you	(May you be well.)
*Kua **mutu***	te ***kura***.	
has finished	the school	(School has finished.)
*Kua **tūreiti***	***au***.	
have become late	I	(I'm late.)

* See Note 3, p. 119.

Stative verbs may also be used (as may action verbs) with the constructions *kei te...* and *i te...*

e.g. *Kei te **pai***	***au!***	
At the being good	I	(I'm fine!)

Stative verbs appear to be of two main types. One type occupies, to some extent, the same position in the Māori language as is occupied in the English language by those whole verbal phrases which consist of some part of the verb 'to be' followed by an adjective.

e.g. ***pai***	be good
tūreiti	to be late
roa	to be long

The other type occupies, to a roughly similar extent, the same position in Māori as is occupied in English by some 'compound tenses' of English verbs — that is, by those whole verbal phrases which consist of some part of the verb 'to be', and/or some part of the verb 'to have', followed by a participle (see below).

e.g. ***mutu***	to be finished (ceased)
mahue	to be left (left behind)
ngaro	to be missing

Participles are words formed from verbs, and used in 'compound' tenses. For example, from the verb 'to finish' are formed the present participle 'finishing' (used in compounds such as 'is finishing' and 'was finishing') and the past participle 'finished' (used in compound tenses such as 'is finished' and 'was finished')*. The words 'finished' and 'esteemed' are examples of English past participles.

In Bruce Biggs' *English•Maori Maori•English Dictionary* the two types of Māori stative verbs are classified as A (adjective) and P (participle) types respectively.†

It should be noted that what distinguishes the 'adjective-type' stative

* Frequently some part of the verb 'to have' will be used in compound tenses in place of, or in addition to, some part of the verb 'to be' (e.g. 'had finished' or 'has been finished').

† In some still current books these types of word are classified as 'adjectives' and 'neuter verbs' ('neuter' because they can have no forms other than that of the past participle) respectively. These terms are considered to be superseded by Bruce Biggs' classification.

verbs from the 'participle-type' is not the type of English words used in their translation*, but the different kinds of use to which they are put in Māori.

Stative verbs of the 'adjective-type' (e.g. ***whero, pai, ora, rangatira***) may be used in the same way as adjectives are used in English, simply to 'qualify' a noun. They are usually placed after the noun they qualify.

e.g. *he* ***whare whero*** (a red house)
te ***reo rangatira*** (the esteemed language)

Perhaps it could be re-emphasized here that although 'adjective-type' stative verbs may be used as adjectives, and although adjectives (plus some part of the verb 'to be') may, in most cases, be used to translate them into English, they are no more adjectives in Māori than are common nouns or action verbs — all of which may, equally, be used as adjectives.

Stative verbs of the 'participle-type' (e.g. ***mutu, mahue***) don't seem to be used, normally, in the manner of adjectives, but only in separate phrases (like participles, in their normal role as parts of verbs, in English).

e.g.	*Kua* ***mutu***	*te* ***kura***.	
	has finished	the school	(School has finished.)
	Kua ***mahue***	*te* ***kurī***.	
	has been left behind	the dog	(The dog's been left behind.)

Most stative verbs may also be used as nouns (e.g. *te* ***pai*** — 'the goodness'; *te* ***ora*** — 'the life and health'; *te* ***roa*** — 'the length'). In some cases noun-endings are added (e.g. *te* ***mutunga*** — 'the finish'). Some stative verbs are perhaps never used as nouns.†

When stative verbs are used with the indefinite article, *he*, the phrase may generally be considered to retain a verbal sense.

* 'Esteemed', for example, is the past participle of 'to esteem', but ***rangatira*** is an A-type stative verb. English participles are, in any case, used as adjectives (e.g. 'an esteemed person').

† See *Let's Learn Maori*, p. 52.

e.g. *He* ***whero*** *te* ***whare.***
is red — the house — (The house is red.)

Sometimes, however, a noun may be the more appropriate translation.

e.g. *He* ***rangatira*** *a* ***Rewi*** (Rewi is a chief.)
(When an action verb is used with *he* the verb has the sense of a noun.)

STATIVE VERBS CHANGED INTO ACTION VERBS BY *WHAKA-*

Stative verbs do not, normally, take passive endings (any 'action' expressed in a stative verb has already a completed, passive sense).

However — stative verbs may be changed into action verbs by the addition of the 'causative' prefix, ***whaka-***. In this form they may take passive endings. (See p. 65.)

e.g. ***whakatūpato*** (***-ria***)	'to cause to be careful', 'to warn'
whakarangatira (***-tia***)	'to cause to be esteemed', 'to ennoble'
whakaroa (***-tia***)	'to cause to be long', 'to lengthen'
whakaora (***-ngia*** or ***-tia***)	'to cause to be healthy', 'to cure'
whakamutu (***-a***)	'to cause to be finished', 'to stop'

As with action verbs, the passive form can be used to give commands.

e.g. ***Whakapaitia*** *te* ***rūma!***	'Tidy the room!'
Whakamutua!	'Stop! (doing something)'

Further Reading

Bruce Biggs' *Let's Learn Maori* established the grammatical theory which distinguishes stative verbs (or, for short, statives) as a class of base word in Māori. The authority remains with that book (rev. ed. 1973) in which relevant sections should be consulted.

It should be noted that neither this theory nor the term 'stative' (nor 'stative verb') have yet been adopted into Williams' dictionary (7th ed. 1971). Stative verbs are, in that essential reference work, classified variously as adjectives, participles and intransitive verbs.

In Bruce Biggs' *English•Maori Maori•English Dictionary* (1990) base words identified as stative verbs are distinguished as such by either A (for adjective-type) or P (for participle-type).

CHAPTER 19

The Modifying of Nouns

An ADJECTIVE is a word (or phrase) which 'names an attribute' — that is, which describes something. When an adjective is placed with a noun it is said to 'modify', or 'qualify', the noun.

In English there is a large number of such words — 'red', 'good', 'big', 'healthy' are simple examples. In English, indeed, adjectives form one of the main classes of base words.

But an adjective is a word which is not able to stand alone as the sole base word in a phrase.* In fact, until comparatively recently what is now called a 'noun' was more fully referred to as a 'noun substantive'; and what is now called an 'adjective' was referred to as a 'noun adjective'. In other words, an 'adjective' is essentially additional to, and dependent upon, a noun.

Adjectives in English may be placed in a phrase with a noun, to 'modify' it (usually preceding the noun).

e.g. A red car
A good house

Theoretically any number of adjectives may be used in any one phrase.

e.g. A good, big, roomy, red house

Alternatively, adjectives may be used with some part of the verb 'to be' to form separate, descriptive, verbal phrases — which serve as counterparts to phrases formed in Māori with stative verbs.

e.g.	The car is red.	(*He **whero***	*te **motokā**.*)
	The rooms were big.	(*He **nui***	*ngā **rūma**.*)

* Although the answer to the question 'What colour is the house?' might be given simply as 'Red.' the balance of a complete sentence — such as 'It is . . .' — is always implied.

Sometimes other 'being' type verbs may be used.

e.g. 'You look healthy.'
'That sounds good.'

In all cases, however, adjectives must stand with some other type of base word.

In Māori it appears that there is no class of words similar to English adjectives. There are certainly words which may be used as adjectives — that is, simply to 'modify' a noun (usually following the noun).

e.g. *te* ***motokā whero*** (the red car)
he ***whare pai*** (a good house)

In fact, most Māori base words may be used in this manner — as the following examples show.

he ***whare kōwhatu*** (a stone house)

Here the COMMON NOUN ***kōwhatu*** (stone) is used as an adjective.

he ***whare kai*** (an eating house)

Here the ACTION VERB ***kai*** (***-nga***) (to eat) is used as an adjective.

he ***whare pai*** (a good house)

Here the STATIVE VERB ***pai*** (to be fine or good) is used as an adjective.

Since common nouns and action verbs, as well as stative verbs, may all be used as adjectives,* there is simply no reason, in Māori, for singling out such words as ***whero, pai, ora*** and ***nui*** to be referred to as 'adjectives' merely because they are used to translate English adjectives.

The reason why such words have been (and in some books still are) called 'adjectives' would seem to be only the quite invalid reason that there are no stative verbs in English!

* The examples also show that in English nouns (e.g. 'stone') and participles of verbs (e.g. 'eating') are used as adjectives.

In Māori a word functioning as an adjective may be one of any of the three main types of base word. Specifically, any COMMON NOUN, any ACTION VERB, or any A-type STATIVE VERB may be used as an adjective.

In English, adjectives usually precede the nouns they modify. In Māori, modifiers (words being used as adjectives) usually follow the noun.

A further difference is that in English several different adjectives may be used in the same phrase.

e.g. 'a good, big house'.

In Māori each different modifier requires a separate phrase. Various types of constructions are used in such situations.

e.g. *he* ***whare pai***	*he* ***nui*** *hoki*
a house good	big also

The modifier itself may, however, be a word-group rather than just a single word.

e.g. *te* ***otaota whai purapura***	
the herb bearing seed	(the seed-bearing herb)
he ***awa wai ora***	
a river water life	(a river of life-giving water)
he ***iringa tāora pepa***	
a hanger towel paper	(a paper-towel rack)

Nouns, as well as verbs, may also be modified by various adverbial particles (see Chapters 21 and 22), and verbs may be modified, as well, by other base words (see p. 66 and Note 3, p. 119).

Chapter 20

Particles 7: Verbal Particles

ka e kua i ana me kia kei (or kai) ina

The verbal particles are words which precede (*ana* is an exception) the verb, usually directly, and which provide information as to how the verb is to be interpreted. Some of these particles have already been considered in previous chapters. A brief resumē is offered here.

ka a new action or state; often used for an action in the future.

e.g.	*Ka* ***haere***	***tātou.***	(Let's go.)
	Ka ***pai***	***tēnā!***	(That's good!)

e may be used on its own for future (though *ka* is often preferred); used in combination with *ana* following the verb (not necessarily directly) for an ongoing action or state — past, present or future — (*ana* may sometimes be replaced by *nei*, *na* or *ra*).

e.g.	*E* ***pai*** *ana*	***au.***	(I'm fine.)
	Te ***whare***	*e* ***tū*** *nei*	(The house, standing here)

kua action has been, or will have been done; state has been arrived at.

e.g.	*Kua* ***haere***	***ia.***	(He/she has gone.)
	Kua ***tūreiti***	***koe***	(You're late.)

i simple past: action was done.

e.g.	*I* ***haere***	***ia.***	(He/she went.)

ana follows the verb, in narrative.

e.g.	***Haere*** *ana*	***rātou.***	(They went.)

also used with *e* (see above) or with *ka* or *kei* preceding the verb.*

me action ought to be done.

* See *Let's Learn Maori*, pp. 95-96.

e.g. *Me* ***haere*** ***tātou.*** (We ought to go.)

kia action or state is desired.

e.g. *... kia* ***haere*** ***koe*** (... that you should go)
Kia ***tūpato!*** (Be careful!)

kei warning — action or state should be avoided.

e.g. *Kei* ***hinga*** ***koe.*** (Don't you fall.) (See also p. 43.)

ina 'if and when' action happens.*

e.g. *Ina* ***haere*** ***koe*** (When you go)

Further Reading

The listing above aims at being only a quick-reference guide for identification of the different verbal particles. The uses of these particles are given wide coverage in several books. A standard reference is the 'Scheme of a Māori verb' on page xxxviii of Williams' dictionary. The uses of *kia* and *kei* especially, in complex sentences, require some careful understanding, for which sections 29, 34 and 36 in *Let's Learn Maori* are very helpful.

Some further comments on verbal phrases in general are given in Chapter 23.

* See *Let's Learn Maori*, p. 35.

CHAPTER 21

Particles 8: Direction Particles

mai atu iho ake

All particles which come after the base word (or words) in a phrase could be described as 'adverbs'. That is, they 'modify' or 'qualify' the base, 'expressing a relation of place, time, circumstance, manner, cause, degree, etc.'* These particles are called 'adverbs' in Williams' dictionary, and, if they are translated into English, they are usually translated by adverbs.

Examples already considered in this book are the three POSITION PARTICLES — *nei, na* and *ra* (see Chapter 24).

The four DIRECTION PARTICLES — *mai, atu, iho* and *ake* — form another small group. All four usually follow (not necessarily directly — another adverb-type particle may intervene) the last base word in a verbal phrase.

e.g.	*E* ***haere*** *mai ana*	*ngā* ***tāngata.***
	moving in this direction	the people
	(The people are coming.)	

mai has almost exactly the same sense as the rather out-of-date English word 'hither' ('in a direction towards the speaker') while *atu* has the sense of 'thither' ('in a direction away from the speaker'). *ake* and *iho* have senses of 'upwards' and 'downwards' respectively.

All four of these particles are frequently used in Māori to give a sense of 'direction' to an action, often when such a sense would not normally be expressed in English.

e.g.	***Kōrero*** *mai*	*ki a* ***au.***	Speak (hither) to me.
	Kōrero *atu*	*ki a* ***Mere.***	Speak (thither) to Mary.
	Inu *mai*	***tāua.***	Let us two drink together.

* *The Concise Oxford Dictionary of Current English.* Eighth edition, ed. R.E. Allen, 1990. This could apply even to the verbal particle *ana.*

Three common action verbs — ***hōmai*** (give hither) ***hoatu*** (give thither) and ***hoake*** ('give or bring elsewhere' or 'go on elsewhere') — are unusual in that the particles are combined with a base that is not used independently. It should also be noted that these words may be used passively but do not take passive endings.

e.g. *I **hōmai***	*te **pukapuka***	*ki a **au**.*
was given	the book	to me

(The book was given to me.)

Other senses of these particles vary according to context. Both *atu* and *ake* may function as 'intensifiers' — that is, they may simply 'intensify' the meaning of another word (usually a stative verb).

e.g. ***pai*** 'to be good'; ***pai*** atu 'to be better'

Further Reading

Several common expressions employ, with various significations, one or other of these particles. The entries for all four in Williams' dictionary should be consulted. Section 21 of *Let's Learn Maori* covers the uses of the these particles very comprehensively.

CHAPTER 22

Particles 9: Other Adverbial Particles

ai anake anō hoki kau kē koa noa pea rawa tonu

The four direction particles of the previous chapter form a concise group. The remainder of the 'adverb-type' particles, listed above (there are other words, also, which could be added to this list) might be described as a very 'mixed bag'.

The uses of some of these particles (e.g. *anake* — 'only') are relatively straight-forward, but the uses of others can be so varied and complex that full description is, as with the uses of prepositions, beyond the scope of this book. (A glance at the entries in Williams' dictionary for *ai*, *anō* or *kē* should be enough to confirm this point.)

Because all of these particles are widely used, however, and all are likely to be frequently encountered (some, such as *ai*, *anō* and *hoki* are used with extreme frequency) it is important that they should at least be identified (and distinguished, in some cases, from base words of identical sound and spelling) and at least some of their uses understood.

All of these particles occur in a position after the base word or words in a phrase (*anō* may also be used before the base).

AI

As with *ko* and the personal article *a*, there is no counterpart in English to this word. It is used in verbal phrases often when the action or state is of regular or 'habitual' occurrence; or where the reason or purpose is given for something being done. Hence is it also used in asking why something is done.

e.g. *He **aha** **koe** i **haere** ai?* (Why did you go?)

Williams' dictionary describes eight different situations in which *ai* is used, with numerous examples. It is doubtful if this information could be put more concisely — and there is no point in simply duplicating that material here. Section 24 of John Foster's *He Whakamārama: A New Course in Māori* also gives good coverage of the use of *ai*.

ANAKE

anake may frequently be translated by 'only'

e.g. *Ko **koe** anake* (You only)

There are several different ways of expressing different senses of 'only' in Māori. If translating from English into Māori, H.M. Ngata's *English-Maori Dictionary* should be consulted.

ANŌ

anō is used with great frequency in a considerable variety of situations and common expressions. Williams' dictionary lists eleven different uses, from the sense of 'again' to that of 'yet' in ***Kāhore** anō* (not yet) and including the reflexive 'self' —

e.g. *Ko **koe** anō* (You yourself)

anō may also occur at the beginning of phrases (see *Let's Learn Maori*, section 41).

HOKI

hoki is one of the most frequently used of all these particles — with the sense either of 'also' or 'because', or simply to give emphasis to a statement (as sometimes 'indeed' is added to remarks in English).

There are also two base words of the same sound and spelling which are widely used. One is ***hoki*** (***-a***) an intransitive action verb with the meaning of 'to go back', 'to return'. (The transitive form ***whakahoki*** (***-a***) — 'to cause to return' — can mean 'to put back', 'to replace' or 'to reply'.) The other word ***hoki*** is the name of a fish (sometimes called 'whiptail'). Thus, the sentence 'I have, indeed, returned the whiptail to Hokianga.' (should it ever be required!) might be rendered —

*Kua **whakahoki** hoki **ahau** i ngā **hoki** ki **Hokianga**.*

(Hokianga is 'the place of return'.)

Frequently, in speech, the particle *hoki* will itself be spoken with considerable emphasis.

KAU

As well as its use as a particle signifying 'alone', 'bare', 'empty' etc. Williams' dictionary lists five separate meanings of ***kau*** as a base word (some of them with more than one application) including ***kau*** (*-**ria***) — 'to swim', and nouns with meanings ranging from 'stalk of a plant' and 'variety of kumara' to 'pupil of the eye' and 'ancestor'.

KĒ

kē generally signifies 'different' or 'other than expected'

e.g.	*Ki te **kōrero***	***tētahi***	*i te **reo** kē...*
	If speaks	someone	in a language different...
	(If any man speak in an unknown tongue...)		

Williams' dictionary distinguishes nine different uses of *kē*.

KOA

Williams' dictionary cites *koā* (though admits *koa* also) with the senses of 'indeed', 'in fact' and 'however'. Also referred to is the use of *koa* 'in entreaty' — sometimes simply as a politeness, with the sense of 'please'.

e.g.	***Hōmai** koa*	*te **parāoa**.*	
	Give hither please	the bread	(Please pass the bread.)

koa is also used in expressions such as ***ahakoa*** (although).

koa (*-**ina***) is an action verb meaning 'to rejoice over'.

NOA

This word presents some problems in terms of classification. Firstly there is the stative verb ***noa***, meaning 'to be common', 'ordinary' or 'free from restriction'. This is the opposite of ***tapu*** (also a stative verb) which means 'to be under ritual restriction'.

Secondly, there is the word *noa* which enters into a variety of constructions in the manner of an adverbial particle (a range of constructions much greater than those in which *tapu* is used). In this case *noa* denotes 'absence of limitations or conditions' — according to Williams' dictionary, which then lists thirteen different applications in this sense.

In Māori many words have multiple meanings, which usually can be clearly distinguished one from the other. For example, *kau*, as a particle signifying 'alone' etc. seems clearly distinguishable from ***kau*** (-***ri***a) — 'to swim'; *hoki*, as a particle signifying 'also', seems only distantly, if at all, connected with ***hoki*** (-***a***) — 'to return'.

In the case of ***noa*** as a stative verb and *noa* as a particle, however, the relationship seems much closer. Williams' dictionary actually lists both under a single head-word — as adjective and adverb respectively. (For further comment on the topic of 'adverb-type' words see Note 2, p. 118.)

PEA

pea has the sense of 'perhaps'. Sometimes, in answer to a question, *pea* may be used just on its own; sometimes with the base word ***āe*** (yes). It may also be used in verb or noun phrases.

e.g. *Ka* ***tika*** *pea* ***tēnā***.
is correct perhaps that
(Perhaps that's correct.)

Ka ***mea*** ***ētahi*** '*He* ***manu*** *pea!*'
said some 'A bird perhaps!'
(Some said 'Perhaps it's a bird!')

RAWA

This is another word which is used to 'intensify' the meaning of the base word (in the same manner as *atu* or *ake*).

e.g. ***pai*** 'to be good' ***pai*** *rawa* 'to be very good'

It can even be used along with *atu* —

e.g. ***pai*** *rawa atu* 'to be exceptionally good'

If the base, ***pai***, is also preceded by ***tino*** (a noun meaning 'essentiality', but which, used descriptively, has the force of 'very') we get:

tino pai *rawa atu* 'to be absolutely marvellous'

It seems (see Williams' dictionary entry for *rawa* (ii). 5.) that this word is also sometimes used as a stative verb meaning 'to be numerous' (*E* ***rawa*** *ana ngā* ***tāngata***.).

Williams' dictionary also records various meanings of ***rawa*** as a noun (entry for ***rawa*** (i), n. 1.-4.) — 'goods', 'property' etc.

TONU

This word signifies 'continuance', and may frequently be translated by 'still' or 'always' — but translation should always be flexible. When called upon to surrender at the battle of Ōrākau in 1864 Rewi Maniapoto is said to have made the famous reply:

'Ka ***whawhai***	*tonu*	***mātou***,	*Ake!*	*Ake!*	*Ake!'*
will fight	on	we,	Ever!	Ever!	Ever!

tonu can also act as an 'intensifier' or with the sense of 'immediately'. It may even be placed between the parts of ***ināianei*** (now) as in ***ināia-tonu-nei*** (immediately).

SUMMARIZING

For a book which purports to be no more than an 'introduction', it might seem that a disproportionately large amount of space has been given here to a small group of words of (in some ways) lesser significance. Most of these words, however, have several applications, and they are used with a frequency as great as, or greater than, the most common base words — so it is useful, even at an introductory level, to have some idea of their functions.

With base words of given meanings, the meanings are more or less constant, for any context. The word ***whare***, for example, always means 'house' (even though it may be used to refer to anything from a dog-kennel to a university); the word ***nui*** always means 'to be big' (whether in size or number).

It is because the adverbial particles, like most particles, do not have any fixed 'meaning' in the manner of base words (*anake* and *pea* could be excepted) that they require more consideration than most other words in a basic vocabulary. It should be also noted that several of these particles may be given the suffix *-tia* when following a passive verb.

With regard to adverbial particles, and 'adverb-type' words in general, some questions of classification remain unresolved. Note 2 on p. 118, provides more comment on this subject.

CHAPTER 23

Verbal Phrases in General

Verbs — both action and stative — may be used in a considerable variety of different types of phrases in Māori — that is, in constructions with a variety of different particles.

The 'Scheme of a Māori verb' at the end of the introduction in Williams' dictionary shows the word ***karanga*** (***-tia***) — 'to call' in more than a dozen types of verbal phrase, most of them with negative as well as affirmative forms. In addition to phrases formed with the verbal particles listed in Chapter 20 (though *ina* is not included) the scheme shows constructions with *me e...*, *me i...* and *ki te...*

Other types of constructions are referred to elsewhere in this book — the uses of *kei te...* (in some areas *kai te...*) and *i te...* (see p. 53) and constructions with *mā* and *nā* (see Chapter 26).

It should be noted that some identical constructions may have more than one possible interpretation, depending on how the phrase in question relates to a sentence as a whole. For instance, *ki te...* may, in one type of situation, have the sense of 'if...'

e.g.	*Ki te* ***karanga***	***ia,***	*ka* ***rongohia***	***āna kupu.***
	If calls	he	would be heard	his words
	(If he calls, his words would be heard.)			

but in another type of situation *ki te...* may have the sense of just 'to' (do something):

e.g.	*I* ***haere***	***ia***	*ki te* ***karanga.***
	went	he	to call
	(He went to call.)		

Such an example shows that the meaning of a phrase such as *ki te* ***karanga*** depends upon its context. This leads to the consideration of more complex sentences in general. What is attempted in this book (in the next chapter) is simply some coverage of some basic types of sentence expansion.

CHAPTER 24

Expanded Sentences — 'Transitive' and 'Intransitive' Verbs and Further uses of the Prepositions *i ki* and *e*

The terms 'transitive' and 'intransitive', in relation to verbs, have been mentioned earlier in this book. Reference has also been made to the 'subject' and 'object' of a sentence.

In simple verbal sentences of two phrases one of the phrases is the verb phrase, and the other is the subject phrase. With an action verb in the ACTIVE form the subject of the sentence is whoever or whatever does the action.

e.g. *I **patu***	***ia.***	
hit	he	(He hit.)
(verb phrase)	(subject phrase)	
*I **haere***	*a **Mere**.*	
went	Mary	(Mary went.)
(verb phrase)	(subject phrase)	

Such sentences may be expanded by the addition of further phrases. It might be wished, for instance, to make statements such as 'He hit the ball.' or 'Mary went to the shop.'

In English, a verb is described as transitive if the action expressed by it passes directly to some 'object' — as in the following:

He	hit	the ball.
(subject phrase)	(verb phrase)	(object phrase)
Rewi	saw	the man.
Mary	knew	the girl.

In such a situation the 'object' is called a direct object.

In English a direct object is always directly 'governed' by a verb, and is not preceded by a preposition.

A sentence with a transitive verb may also be expanded by a phrase beginning with a preposition, which introduces an indirect object.

e.g. He hit the ball *into* the trees.
(indirect object)

An indirect object is usually (but not invariably) introduced by a preposition.

If there is no passing of action to a direct object the verb is described as intransitive.

e.g. Mary went.
He is running.

Such sentences may also be expanded by a phrase beginning with a preposition.

e.g. Mary went *to* the shop.'

(In this case, what is introduced by the preposition is not called an 'object', since 'objects', whether direct or indirect, are considered to belong only with transitive verbs.)

Turning to Māori, the following sentences may be considered:

I ***patu***	***ia***	*i te* ***paoro.***	
hit	he	the ball	(He hit the ball.)
I ***kite*** *a*	***Rewi***	*i te* ***tangata.***	
saw	Rewi	the man	(Rewi saw the man.)
I ***mōhio***	*a* ***Mere***	*ki te* ***kōtiro.***	
knew	Mary	the girl	(Mary knew the girl.)
I ***haere***	*a* ***Mere***	*ki te* ***toa.***	
went	Mary	to the shop	(Mary went to the shop).

*I **haere***	*a **Rewi***	*i te **toa**.*	
went	Rewi	from the shop	(Rewi went from the shop.)

It can be seen that in all the Māori sentences the added phrase is joined to the sentence by a preposition. It might therefore be asked what distinction does actually exist in Māori between such sentences as the following:

*I **mōhio***	*a **Mere***	*ki te **kōtiro**.*	
knew	Mary	the girl	(Mary knew the girl.)

and

*I **haere***	*a **Mere***	*ki te **toa**.*	
went	Mary	to the shop	(Mary went to the shop.)

It might be asked whether terms such as 'transitive', 'intransitive', 'direct object' and 'indirect object', have, in fact, any application to Māori.

But what is expressed in these terms ('transitive', 'intransitive' etc.) does seem really to exist in life — that is, some actions directly affect objects and that some objects are affected only indirectly (whatever language is being used) — and the terms used to distinguish the difference can be of some help in understanding at least some of the uses of prepositions in Māori.

It may be said, for instance, that, in Māori, the 'object' of the action of a verb is normally* introduced by a preposition, as in all of the example sentences on the previous page. This means that a preposition is used even when the 'object' is directly affected by the action (i.e. is a direct object of a transitive verb) as in the first three examples.

These three examples also show that a direct object may be introduced by either *i* or *ki*. The basic rule appears to be that for most 'transitive' verbs in Māori a direct object is connected by the preposition *i*.

* But see also pp. 104-105.

e.g.	*I* ***patu***	***ia***	*i te* ***paoro.***
	I ***kite***	*a* ***Rewi***	*i te* ***tangata.***

and

Ka ***waiata***	*te* ***kōtiro***	*i te* ***waiata.***	
sings	the girl	the song	(The girl sings the song.)
Me ***whāngai***	*a* ***Rewi***	*i ngā* ***kāwhe.***	
Ought to feed	Rewi	the calves	(Rewi ought to feed the calves.)
I ***tuhituhi***	*a* ***Mere***	*i ngā* ***kupu.***	
wrote	Mary	the words	(Mary wrote the words.)

Some action verbs however, which would seem to be 'transitive', have (what would seem to be) direct objects connected by *ki*.

e.g.	*I* ***mōhio***	*a* ***Mere***	*ki te* ***kōtiro.***

and

Ka ***aroha***	***au***	*ki a* ***koe.***	
love	I	you	(I love you.)

With plenty of practice these constructions are not so very difficult to memorise.

e.g.	***whāngai*** *. . . .*	*i . . .*
	tuhituhi *. . . .*	*i . . .*

but

mōhio *. . . .*	*ki . . .*
aroha *. . . .*	*ki . . .**

It must be remembered that the reference here is to transitive verbs and to direct objects only (which, in English, do not have prepositions) and that transitive verbs may also take indirect objects.

* A useful listing of common verbs which take *ki* will be found on pp. 49-50 of *Making Maori Sentences*.

e.g. *I **tuhituhi*** *a Mere* *i ngā **kupu**.*
wrote Mary the words

(Mary wrote the words.) (direct object)

but

*I **tuhituhi*** *a Mere* *ki te **kōtiro**.*
wrote Mary to the girl
(Mary wrote to the girl.) (indirect object)

* * * *

In English there is a large number of prepositions — such as 'at', 'by', 'from', 'in', 'of', 'on', 'to', 'with', to mention just a few of them. In Māori, two prepositions in particular* — i, and ki — perform a whole range of functions similar to several of the functions of all these English prepositions, and more.

It is not a simple matter of any one Māori preposition covering all the uses of any one, or several, English prepositions. The Māori system of prepositions, rather (as has been said of the verb constructions) cuts obliquely across the English system.

To understand the use of prepositions in Māori, the Māori context needs to be considered quite independently of what preposition may be appropriate in English.

Some of the uses of *i* and *ki* may, in this manner, be relatively easy to follow. For example, after action verbs of motion (intransitive) such as ***haere*** (***-a***) — 'to go (or come)' and ***oma*** (***-kia***) 'to run' the preposition *ki* has the sense of 'to' or 'towards'

e.g. *I **haere*** *a Mere* *ki te **toa**.*
went Mary to the shop

and the preposition *i* has the sense of 'from'.†

e.g. *I **haere*** *a Mere* *i te **toa**.*
went Mary from the shop

* Other prepositions, which may, in various contexts, translate one or more of the listed English prepositions (but the uses of which are not as complicated as those of *i* and *ki*) are disregarded for the moment.

† Or sometimes 'by way of' or 'in company with'. See Williams' dictionary entries: I (ii), prep. 2, 10 and 16.

It could be said that *ki* may be taken to express a sense of 'to' or 'towards' generally — just as much with verbs such as ***aroha*** (***-ina***) and ***mōhio*** (***-tia***) as with verbs such as ***haere*** (***-a***), ***oma*** (***-kia***) or ***titiro*** (***tirohia***) — whatever preposition, if any, is used in English translation.

This generalisation, however, doesn't really cover some of the uses of *ki* — such as in *ki te*... meaning 'if...', or the use of *ki* as the preposition for the 'instrument' (the 'thing' with which something is done).

e.g. ***Tuhia***	*ki te* ***pene***	*ki te* ***mangumangu.***	
Write	with pen	with ink	(Write with pen and ink.)

(This last example also shows how, in Māori, the preposition should be repeated, creating a separate phrase for each object.)

The uses of *i* are even more varied than those of *ki*. Some of these uses have already been referred to. Further information follows in the next few pages.

* * * *

So far, in this chapter, the verbs considered have been exclusively ACTION VERBS, used in the active form. Some brief notes now follow regarding the expansion of sentences with ACTION VERBS in the passive form, and, later, of sentences with STATIVE VERBS.

SENTENCES USING ACTION VERBS IN THE PASSIVE

With an action verb in the PASSIVE form, the subject of the sentence is whoever or whatever the action is done to.

e.g. *I* ***tuhia***	*ngā* ***kupu***	
were written	the words	(The words were written.)
(verb phrase)	(subject phrase)	
Ka ***arohaina***	*te* ***kōtiro.***	
is loved	the girl	(The girl is loved.)
(verb phrase)	(subject phrase)	

Sentences such as these are commonly expanded by an AGENT PHRASE — that is a phrase explaining by whom or what (i.e. by the agency of whom or what) the action (to the subject) is done.

The preposition in this case is *e*.

e.g.	*I* ***tuhia***	*ngā* ***kupu***	*e* ***Mere****.*
	were written	the words	by Mary
	(verb phrase)	(subject phrase)	(agent phrase)

(The words were written by Mary.)

Ka ***arohaina***	*te* ***kōtiro***	*e te* ***tamaiti****.*
is loved	the girl	by the child
(verb phrase)	(subject phrase)	(agent phrase)

(The girl is loved by the child.)

It could be mentioned here that the passive form is used much more frequently in Māori than in English. Striking examples of this are found throughout *Ko te Paipera Tapu* (*The Holy Bible*). Sentences are frequently in passive form in Māori where, in the Authorised King James English version (which the Māori text closely parallels) the English verbs are in active form.

e.g.	*Ka* ***huaina***	*te* ***kikorangi***	*e te* ***Atua***
	was called	the firmament	by God

ko te ***Rangi****.*
the Heaven
(God called the firmament Heaven.)

Ka ***whakakitea*** *mai*	*e* ***ia***	*ki* ***ahau***
was shown	by him	to me

he ***awa wai ora****.*
a river (of) water living
(He showed me a river of water of life.)

Sentences with Stative Verbs

When a sentence with a stative verb is expanded by an agent phrase the preposition (by contrast) is *i*.

e.g.	*Ka **ora***	*te **tangata***	*i te **rongoa**.*
	becomes well	the man	by (agency of) the medicine

The example above is given in *Let's Learn Maori* (p. 30) to show clearly the necessity of distinguishing between stative verbs and action verbs.

With a transitive action verb *i* simply introduces a direct object.

e.g.	*Ka **inu***	*te **tangata***	*i te **rongoa**.*
	drinks	the man	the medicine
	(The man drinks the medicine.)		

With an intransitive action verb of motion *i* may signify 'from', 'via' or 'in company with'.

e.g.	*I **haere** mai*	***ia***	*i **Otepoti**.*
	came	he	from Dunedin
	(He came from Dunedin.)		

With a stative verb *i* signifies 'by (agency of)'.

e.g.	*Ka **ora***	*te **tangata***	*i te **rongoa**.*
	is made well	the man	by the medicine
	(The man is made well by the medicine.)		

With an action verb in the passive form *e* is used to signify 'by (agency of)'.

e.g.	*Ka **inumia***	*te **rongoa***	*e te **tangata**.*
	is drunk	the medicine	by the man
	(The medicine is drunk by the man.)		

Further Reading

The examples given in this chapter by no means exhaust the various uses of *i*, *ki* and *e* (as a study of the entries for these prepositions in Williams' dictionary clearly shows). When translating from English into Māori the *English-Maori Dictionary* by H.M. Ngata offers the appropriate words for the different English prepositions in different contexts.

The study of more complex sentences may be pursued further, in practice, in the books of the *Te Rangatahi* series and in *Te Reo Rangatira* (as well as in *Let's Learn Maori*).

Ideally, at least some form of practice (listening, conversing, reading, writing) should become a daily habit! Written material for such practice ranges from children's stories to such classical Māori texts as *Ngā Mahi a Ngā Tūpuna* and *Ngā Kōrero a Mohi Ruatapu*. Further suggestions are given in the bibliography of this book.

Chapter 25

Possessives

The prepositions *a, o, nā, nō, mā* and *mō*, and the possessive particles *tā, tō, ā* and *ō* have been given brief coverage in Chapters 11 and 13. All of these particles are used in Māori to express the idea of some thing or person belonging to, or being possessed by another. This topic is considered more fully here.

One of the common ways of expressing 'belonging' (remembering that in Māori there are two categories — *a* and *o* — of possession*) is shown in the following:

ngā ***pukapuka***	*a* ***Mere***	
the books	of Mary	(the books belong to Mary)
te ***whaea***	*o* ***Mere***	
the mother	of Mary	(the mother belongs to Mary)
te ***kakau***	*o te* ***kapu***	
the handle	of the cup	(the handle belongs to the cup)

The above type of construction is very widely used in Māori, but in English, in the first two examples at least, it is somewhat less than usual. The preferred construction would be 'Mary's books' and 'Mary's mother'. These phrases (and even the last example could be rendered as 'the cup's handle') use what is called the Possessive Case of nouns.

The possessive case of a noun is formed, in English (as the above examples show) by adding an apostrophe and the letter 's' to the noun. Thus 'Mary's' is the possessive case of 'Mary'; and 'cup's' is the possessive case of 'cup'.

* See p.49.

In Māori nouns don't change to form cases. Possessive cases — or (for short) POSSESSIVES — of nouns in Māori are formed simply by placing one of the particles *tā, tō, ā, ō, nā, nō, mā* or *mō* before the noun.

The possessive particles *tā* and *tō* (and their plurals *ā* and *ō*) form what could be called 'simple' possessives.

e.g. *tō* ***Mere whaea*** (Mary's mother)
ā ***Mere pukapuka*** (Mary's books)

This type of construction is probably not as common in Māori as the former type (*te* ***whaea*** *o* ***Mere*** and *ngā* ***pukapuka*** *a* ***Mere***) and such a construction as *'tō te* ***kapu kakau****'* would presumably be rare (usually it would be *te* ***kakau*** *o te* ***kapu***).

The particles *tā, tō, ā* and *ō*, however, have great importance in forming simple possessives with the personal pronouns.

In English, possessive 'cases' are not formed by adding "s' to the pronouns. Instead, there are two sets of quite distinct words. Firstly, the SIMPLE POSSESSIVES, as follows:

SIMPLE POSSESSIVES		
	Singular	Plural
1st person	my	our
2nd person	your	your
3rd person	his/her	their

These simple possessives are not, in themselves, pronouns, since they cannot stand alone in phrases.

In Māori possessives are formed with the personal pronouns (just as they are with nouns) simply by placing a possessive particle before the pronoun.

Thus, *tō* ***mātou***, for example, literally means 'belonging to us' (that is, 'our') *ō* ***koutou*** literally means 'belonging to you' (that is, 'your').

e.g. *tō* ***mātou matua*** (our father)
ō ***koutou tūpuna*** (your ancestors)

The distinction between *ā* and *ō* categories of possession also applies —

e.g. *ō* ***rātou tūpuna*** (their ancestors)
ā ***rātou kurī*** (their dogs)

It can be seen, then, that Māori really requires two words (a possessive particle and a pronoun) to give a meaning corresponding to that of an English single-word possessive. This is true for all the forms for two people and three or more people.

In the forms for one person, however, a radical change takes place. The possessive particles are not placed before ***au***, ***koe*** or ***ia***. Instead, these three words change to ***ku***, ***u*** and ***na*** respectively, and the possessive particle is placed before these (and the combination is usually written as one word).

e.g. *tā**ku*** ***pukapuka*** (my book)
*ō**u*** ***hū*** (your shoes)
*tō**na*** ***pōtae*** (his or her hat)

In addition, it needs to be mentioned that while some speakers maintain distinct *ā* and *ō* forms for one person, other speakers use 'neutral' forms which don't make this distinction (n.b. this applies only to forms for one person).

These 'neutral' forms are shown in brackets in the following complete scheme of the one person simple possessives.

SINGULAR (ONE PERSON) SIMPLE POSSESSIVES		
	Singular 1 thing owned	Plural 2+ things owned
1st person	my ***tāku*** ***(taku)*** ***tōku***	my ***āku*** ***(aku)*** ***ōku***
2nd person	your ***tāu*** *(tō)* ***tōu***	your ***āu*** *(ō)* ***ōu***
3rd person	his/her ***tāna*** ***(tana)*** ***tōna***	his/her ***āna*** ***(ana)*** ***ōna***

The so-called 'neutral' forms (for one person only) may be used for any type of article or property possessed.

e.g. *taku* ***kurī*** (my dog)
taku ***pōtae*** (my hat)
aku ***hū*** (my shoes)

An important difference between the English 'simple' possessives and these Māori 't-class' possessives is that the latter may 'stand alone', in an alternative use:

e.g. *He* ***kurī*** *tāku.* (I have a dog.)

* * * *

Consideration, so far, has been given only to 'simple' possessives. In English, there are also what is called 'absolute' possessives.

The form of an absolute possessive of a noun is the same as the simple possessive (''s' added to the noun). The difference is in how the word is used. The absolute possessive stands in a separate phrase, detached from the thing it possesses. The following examples should make clear what is meant.

SIMPLE POSSESSIVE: 'Mary's book is on the table.'

ABSOLUTE POSSESSIVE: 'The book on the table is Mary's.'

The absolute possessives of personal pronouns are words which (like absolute possessives of nouns) 'stand alone' — they are POSSESSIVE PRONOUNS:

ABSOLUTE POSSESSIVES (PRONOUNS)		
	Singular	Plural
1st person	mine	ours
2nd person	yours	yours
3rd person	his/hers	theirs

These words are used in the same manner as the absolute possessives of nouns —

e.g. 'The book on the table is hers.'

Comparable senses of possession are expressed in Māori by the use of prepositions, as follows:

NĀ AND *NŌ*

The prepositions *nā* and *nō* are used to form possessives which signify 'belonging to, by right of ownership established in the past'.

As possessives formed with *tā, tō, ā* and *ō* are counterparts to English simple possessives, so these, with *nā* and *nō*, are counterparts to the English absolute possessive cases.

e.g. *Nā **Mere***	*te **pukapuka***	*kei **runga***	*i te **tēpu**.*
Mary's	the book	upon	the table

(The book on the table is Mary's.)

With both personal names and personal pronouns, *nā* and *nō* form possessives in exactly the same way as *tā* and *tō* (but there is no neutral form and no change to a plural for things possessed). All are counterparts to English absolute possessives.

e.g. *Nō**ku***	***tērā pōtae.***	
Mine	that hat	(That hat is mine.)
*Nā **rātou***	***ērā kurī***	
Theirs	those dogs	(Those dogs are theirs.)

MĀ AND *MŌ*

The prepositions *mā* and *mō* are used to form possessives which signify 'belonging to, by right of ownership to be established in the future'. There is no 'case' in English as counterpart to these constructions. Usually 'for...' is an appropriate translation.

Possessives are formed with *mā* and *mō* in an identical manner to those with *nā* and *nō* (no neutral form and no change for plural of things possessed).

e.g. *Mā **Mere***	***ēnei pukapuka.***	
for Mary	these books	(These books are for Mary.)
*Mō **rātou***	***tērā whare.***	
for them	that house	(That house is for them.)
*He **kapu tī***	***māu?***	
A cup of tea	for you?	(Would you like a cup of tea?)

Further Reading

A chart of the personal pronouns (such as that on p. 29) may usefully be matched with the eight particles (*tā, tō, ā, ō, nā, nō, mā* and *mō*) which are placed before them to form the possessives — remembering that ***au, koe,*** and ***ia*** change to ***ku, u*** and ***na*** respectively, and the combinations of these with particles are written as one word. (The only real irregularity is that of the 'neutral' forms *ta**ku**, tō* etc.)

It can be seen that, with four different possibilities in Māori for 'us' (***tāua, māua, tātou, mātou***) and eight different particles to place before each, there are thirty-two possible variations for the one English word 'our'. Some careful thinking is therefore probably required by the English-speaker — until familiarity is gained with all the variables which need to be taken into account.

Another function of the possessives formed with *nā* and *mā* is the subject of the next chapter.

CHAPTER 26

Emphasis on the 'Actor'

In the previous chapter the focus has been on the 'possession' or 'ownership' of things or persons. There is, however, a particular type of construction in Māori which expresses, in a sense, the 'ownership' of actions. In *Let's Learn Maori* this is called the 'actor-emphatic' construction.

The term 'actor' probably most commonly suggests the idea of a stage or film 'actor'. Here the word is used simply in its basic sense of a person who does an action. Thus, in the following sentence it is Mere who is the 'actor':

e.g *Ka **haere*** *a **Mere**.* (Mary goes.)

In the next sentence *'te **tangata**'* is the 'actor':

e.g. *Kei te **waiata*** *te **tangata**.* (The man is singing.)

In the following ***rātou*** is the 'actor' (or perhaps it should be 'are the actors'):

e.g.	*I **horoi***	***rātou***	*i ngā **rīhi**.*	
	washed	they	the dishes	(They washed the dishes.)

The 'actor' in a sentence is thus also the 'subject' of the sentence.

It has previously been shown how the subject may be emphasized by shifting it to the beginning of the sentence and introducing it with *ko* (see pp. 47-49).

e.g.	*Ko **Rewi***	*kei te **hanga***	*i te **whare**.*
	Rewi	is building	the house.

This construction may be used for past, present or future. It should be noted also that the 'object' (what is 'acted upon') is still introduced by a preposition.

In the following 'actor-emphatic' types of construction the emphasis is placed upon the 'actor', with the implication that the action (in a sense) actually 'belongs to' whoever did it or who will do it.

It should be remembered that transitive actions are (in relation to the 'doer') governed by *a*-class possessives (see p. 50).

Thus, the possessives formed with *nā* are used in constructions which emphasise who did something in the past. (The verbal particle used is *i*.)

e.g.	*Nā **Rewi***	*i **horoi***	*ngā **rīhi**.*
	Rewi	washed	the dishes.
	Nāna	*i **whāngai***	*ngā **kāwhe**.*
	He/she	fed	the calves.
	*Nā **mātou***	*i **hanga***	*te **whare**.*
	We	built	the house.

The possessives formed with *mā* are used in constructions which emphasize who will do something in the future. (The verbal particle used is *e*.)

e.g.	*Mā **Mere***	*e **horoi***	*ngā **rīhi**.*
	Mary	will wash	the dishes.
	Māku	*e **kī** atu*	
	I	will say.	
	*Mā **tātou***	*e **hanga***	*te **whare**.*
	We	will build	the house.

Because, in the *nā* and *mā* constructions the 'object' of the action of the verb is not preceded by a preposition (in contrast to the construction with *ko*) it may be considered that these constructions are similar in some ways to passive constructions — where what is 'acted upon' becomes the subject of the sentence (although the verb here remains in the active form).

e.g.	*Nā **Rewi***	*i **hanga***	*te **whare**.*	
	By Rewi	was built	the house	(The house was built by Rewi.)

*Mā **māua***	*e **horoi***	*ngā **rīhi**.*	
By us	will be washed	the dishes	(The dishes will be washed by us.)

Linguists appear to be divided in opinions on this issue. In practice, all that really needs to be remembered is that, in these constructions, what is 'acted upon' is not preceded by a preposition.

Further Reading

Section 24 in *Let's Learn Maori* considers these constructions. Particular notice should be paid to 24.3 (p. 74) of that book, in which a construction using *nō ... e ... ana* is discussed.

CHAPTER 27

Negatives

A 'negative', in terms of grammar, is a word, phrase or sentence which expresses 'denial, prohibition or refusal'.*

The simplest form of negative in English is the single word 'No' — for which Māori has counterparts in ***Kāo*** and ***Kāhore*** (in some areas ***Kāore***).

Negative sentences may be regarded as 'transforms' of affirmative sentences. The negative 'transforms' of most types of verbal sentences are given in the 'Scheme of a Māori verb' at the end of the introduction in Williams' dictionary.

e.g.	Affirmative			
	*E **karanga** ana*	***ia***.	(He was, is, or will be calling.)	
	Negative			
	Kāhore	***ia***	*e **karanga** ana.*	(He was not, is not, or will not be calling.)
	Affirmative			
	*I **karanga***	***ia***.	(He called.)	
	Negative			
	Kīhai	***ia***	*i **karanga**.*	(He did not call.)

The pattern which can be observed is that in negative sentences the sentence is begun with the 'negation' phrase and then the usual order of verb/subject is reversed.

e.g.	*I **karanga***	***ia***.	(He called.)	
	(verb)	(subject)		
	Kīhai	***ia***	*i **karanga**.*	(He did not call.)
	(negation)	(subject)	(verb)	

With some constructions other changes also occur —

* *The Concise Oxford Dictionary of Current English.* Eighth edition. ed. R.E. Allen, 1990.

The particle *kua* is, for the negative, replaced by *kia*, and *anō* is frequently added to the negation phrase.

e.g. *Kua* ***karanga***	***ia.***	(He had, has, or will have called.)
Kāhore *(anō)*	*kia* ***karanga ia.***	(He has not, had not, or will have not called (yet).)

The particle *ka* (which, in the affirmative, has no defined time-signification) is often replaced in the negative by (according to which is appropriate) the past negative construction (***Kīhai***... *i*...) or the future negative construction (*E* ***kore***... *e*...).

e.g. *E* ***kore*** ***ia*** *e* ***karanga.*** (He will not call.)

For a negative 'imperative' — that is, a command not to do something (this applies only with action verbs) the construction used is ***Kaua*** (sometimes ***Kauaka***) *e*...

e.g. ***Kaua*** *e* ***karanga!*** (Don't call!)

For nominal (that is noun, or non-verbal) sentences the negatives are formed as follows:

For sentences beginning with either *kei* or *i* the negative used is ***kāhore.*** However, *kei* is not used in the negative, and must be replaced by *i.*

e.g. *Kei te* ***whare***	*a* ***Rewi.***	(Rewi is at the house.)	
Kāhore	*a* ***Rewi***	*i te* ***whare.***	(Rewi is not, or was not, at the house.)

For sentences beginning with *ko, he, na, no, ma* or *mo* the negative is formed with ***ehara.***

A phrase beginning with *nā, nō, mā* or *mō* may be converted to the negative simply by placing ***ehara*** at the beginning, and no other changes are required in the sentence.

e.g. *Nā* ***Mere***	***tērā pukapuka.***		(That book is Mary's.)
Ehara	*nā* ***Mere***	***tērā pukapuka.***	(That book is not Mary's.)

Nōku	***tēnei pōtae.***		(This hat is mine.)
Ehara	*nōku*	***tēnei pōtae.***	(This hat is not mine.)

The same principle also applies to 'actor-emphatic' verbal sentences.

e.g. *Mā **rātou***	*e **horoi***	*ngā **rīhi.***	(They will wash the dishes.)	
Ehara	*mā **rātou***	*e **horoi***	*ngā **rīhi.***	(They will not wash the dishes.)

For sentences beginning with *ko* or *he* however other changes are required, as shown in the following:

e.g. *Ko **Rewi***	*te **tangata.***		(Rewi is the man.)
Ehara	a ***Rewi***	i te ***tangata.***	(Rewi is not the man.)
*He **whero***	*te **whare.***		(The house is red.)
Ehara	*te **whare***	*i te **whero.***	(The house is not red.)

These changes (*ko* is changed to *a*; the preposition *i* is introduced; and *he* is changed to *te*) may be explained by Bruce Biggs' comment in *Let's Learn Maori* (p. 76) that the negation words — ***kāhore*** and ***ehara*** — can be understood as verbal phrases (*ka **hore*** and *e **hara*** respectively — just as the future negative is usually written *e **kore***).

This means that when nominal sentences such as —

*Kei te **whare** a **Rewi*** and *Ko **Rewi** te **tangata.***

are changed into the negative they are actually converted into verbal sentences, and thus follow the normal pattern of simple verbal sentences:

Kāhore	*a **Rewi***	*i te **whare.***
is not	Rewi	at the house
(verb phrase)	(subject phrase)	(object phrase)
Ehara	*a **Rewi***	*i te **tangata.***
is not	Rewi	the man
(verb phrase)	(subject phrase)	(object phrase)

The suggestion could be made then, that, although in Māori there may not be any verb 'to be', there is a verb 'to not be'. (This would apply in particular to ***hore***. The stative verb ***hara*** actually means 'to be wrong'.)

Further Reading

Negatives can be confusing, and variations to the patterns given above may well be encountered. A handy, concise guide may be found in *Teach Yourself Māori* (pp. 59-61).

For fuller information sections 20 and 25 of *Let's Learn Maori* should be consulted.

CHAPTER 28

Summarizing

A phrase in Māori consists of one or more base words, sometimes with particles before, after, or in both places.

There are three main types of base word —

NOUNS • ACTION VERB • STATIVE VERB

There are three main types of noun —

COMMON NOUNS	(names of things — e.g. ***rākau, whare, ika***)
PERSONAL NOUNS	(names of people, and personal names given to things)
LOCATION NOUNS	(names of locations — e.g. ***runga waho, konei*** — and all place-names)

The location nouns — apart from place-names — consist of a relatively small, 'closed' set (that is, normally no new words are added).

Also to be considered with nouns are the DEFINITIVE PRONOUNS (e.g. ***tēnei, tētahi***) and the PERSONAL PRONOUNS (***au, koe, koutou*** etc.). These sub-classes are also 'closed' sets, and should be learnt in their entirety.

ACTION VERBS may be used in both ACTIVE and PASSIVE forms. For the latter, a passive ending is added to the base.

STATIVE VERBS are of two types — A (adjective)-type and P (participle)-type.

Nouns are words which are not used as verbs, but all action verbs and most stative verbs may be used as nouns. Frequently a noun-ending is added to the base.

All common nouns, action verbs and A-type stative verbs may (without any alteration) be used as adjectives — that is, to 'qualify' or 'modify' nouns (or other base words used as nouns). The modifier usually follows the noun.

Particles may be seen to belong to different groups —

ARTICLES

PREPOSITIONS

POSSESSIVE PARTICLES

VERBAL PARTICLES

ADVERBIAL PARTICLES

Action verbs and stative verbs, but not nouns, may be used as sole base words in phrases with verbal particles.

Two particles in particular have no counterparts in English:— *ko* (the 'focus' particle) and *a* (the personal article, used before personal nouns and pronouns and location nouns in some situations).

Several other particles — particularly the prepositions — have multiple uses (requiring different interpretations in different contexts).

The particles (about 60 in total) are also a 'closed' set of words — and their various uses should also be learnt in their entirety.

THE STRUCTURE OF SENTENCES

In Māori the simplest sentence consists of just a single verbal phrase.

e.g. *Ka **ahiahi**.* (It becomes evening.)

Most sentences, however, consist of two or more phrases.

The common order of phrases in a sentence is —

VERB PHRASE • SUBJECT PHRASE • OBJECT PHRASE

e.g. *I **whāngai***	*a **Mere***	*i te **tamaiti**.*
fed	Mary	the child

If the subject is to be emphasized it may be placed at the beginning of the sentence, introduced by the 'focus' particle *ko*:

e.g.	*Ko* ***Mere***	*i* ***whāngai***	*i te* ***tamaiti.***
	Mary	fed	the child

(It was Mary who fed the child.)

Passive constructions are used more frequently in Māori than in English.

e.g.	*I* ***whāngaia***	*te* ***tamaiti***	*e* ***Mere.***
	was fed	the child	by Mary

Alternative constructions, emphasizing the 'actor', are formed using the preposition *na* (with *i* before the verb) for past actions, and the preposition *ma* (with *e* before the verb) for future actions.

e.g.	*Na* ***Mere***	*i* ***whāngai***	*te* ***tamaiti.***
	Mary	fed	the child
	Ma ***Mere***	*e* ***whāngai***	*te* ***tamaiti.***
	Mary	will feed	the child

In Māori there is no equivalent to the English verb 'to be'. Its place is to a large extent occupied by Māori STATIVE VERBS, which frequently correspond to English constructions consisting of some part of the verb 'to be' with an adjective or participle.

In English two noun phrases are commonly joined by the verb 'to be' to form a complete sentence.

e.g. Rewi *is* the man.

In Māori, however, sentences may be complete without any verb. Two noun phrases may simply be placed together.

e.g. *Ko* ***Rewi*** *te* ***tangata.***

Negative sentences are formed by placing a 'negation phrase' at the beginning of a sentence and reversing the usual verb-subject order.

e.g.	***Kīhai***	*a* ***Mere***	*i* ***whāngai***	*i te* ***tamaiti.***

(Mary did not feed the child.)

Negation words are verbal phrases, and may be seen as converting verbless sentences into verbal sentences.

e.g. ***Ehara***	*a* ***Rewi***	*i te* ***tangata.***	
is not	Rewi	the man	(Rewi is not the man.)
VERB	SUBJECT	OBJECT	

(This suggests that, although there may be no equivalent in Māori of the English verb 'to be', there are verbs — the negation words — which carry the sense of 'to not be'.)

Although this summary is necessarily short on detail, the application of the principles outlined should (with the use of a dictionary!) allow reasonable success in understanding most passages of Māori.

There are always pitfalls, however, and in any case (as stressed in the preface) 'understanding' is not the same as fluency. Fluency is to be achieved by practice, correction, and more practice.

CHAPTER 29

Pronunciation Guide

Good pronunciation of Māori should be achieved by careful listening, much practice, and correction by native speakers. A guide such as this may be of some aid in understanding the basic principles only.

In the written form of Māori the alphabet now usually employed consists of 15 'letters', comprised of —

5 VOWELS

a *e* *i* *o* *u*

8 SINGLE LETTER CONSONANTS

h *k* *m* *n* *p* *r* *t* *w*

2 DIGRAPH CONSONANTS

ng *wh*

VOWEL SOUNDS

In written English, none of the five vowel letters are limited to one specific sound. For example, the sounds for the letter 'a' are quite different in 'bat', 'bath' and 'bathe'.

In Māori, by contrast, each letter represents only one sound. There are thus only five single vowel sounds recognised in Māori. Each of these sounds, however, may be pronounced 'long' or 'short'.

A rough guide to these sounds, in terms of English words, might be given as follows:

LONG	SHORT
ā as in father	*a* as in about
ē as in bread	*e* as in bred
ī as in machine	*i* as in igloo
ō as in board	*o* as in report
ū as in rule	*u* as in put

The practice of indicating that a vowel is long by placing a macron (¯)

over the letter now seems to have become standard. In some texts, however, vowel-length may not be indicated — e.g. in the currently available text of *Ko te Paipera Tapu* (the Māori bible). In other texts long vowels may be shown by a doubling of the letter (as in Bruce Biggs' books).

Correct vowel-length is important in Māori for determining the meaning of words. In many cases words of quite different meaning are distinguished one from the other only by the length of a vowel.

Even when the macron system is used (as in this book) some words will have double vowels. These are words probably compounded from two words put together, or words beginning with ***a*** which are prefixed with whaka-

e.g. ***mata***	+	***atua***	→	***Mataatua***	(name of a canoe)
whaka-	+	***aro***	→	***whakaaro (-tia)***	(to think)

Wherever doubled vowels occur they are pronounced as single long sounds. Each of these single sounds, whether long or short, is a pure vowel sound — that is, a sound which can be prolonged without changing.

Where one vowel sound follows another (different) vowel sound so smoothly that virtually a single syllable is formed the pair of vowel sounds is called a diphthong.

In English, diphthong sounds are often represented simply by single vowel letters. For example, the 'a' in 'bathe' and the 'o' in 'go' are both diphthongs. In English (particularly in some accents) diphthongs frequently sound rather harsh and 'impure'.

In Māori, diphthong sounds always consist of the correct ('pure') pronunciation of each of the vowels — and each is designated by a letter in writing.

With any pair of vowels, the transition from one sound to the next should always be as smooth as possible. Some pairs (e.g. *ia* and *ua*) may sound as two syllables, while with other pairs (e.g. *au* and *ou*) virtually a single syllable is formed.

When several vowels occur in sequence they are paired into 'syllables' according to where the smoothest transition is possible.

e.g. ***uaua*** is pronounced ***u-au-a*** (not ***u-a-u-a)***

This rule applies even across from one word to another.

e.g. *Kia* ***ora!*** is pronounced *Ki-ao-**ra!*** (not *Ki-a-**o-ra**!*)

If vowel-pairs are accepted as single syllables (diphthongs) it may be stated that a syllable in Māori consists of either a single vowel, or a pair of vowels, or a consonant followed by either a single vowel or a vowel-pair. (Examples of syllables would thus be: *a, ā, āe, ha, hā, hau* etc.).

CONSONANTS

Although some authorities recommend refinement of the *p* and *t* sounds, pronunciation as in English is generally considered acceptable for all the single-letter consonants — with the notable exception of *r*.

The *r* should not be 'rolled' — that is, the tongue should not be curled up, but should remain flat, and 'tap' as in the formation of 'd' or 'l'. (Several books printed early in the previous century used d in words where r is now standard. In the south, it appears that the sound heard by Europeans seemed closer to 'l' and place-names on maps still record this, e.g. ***Waihola*** and ***Kilmog*** — a variation of ***Kirimoko***.)

The digraph *ng* can initially cause some difficulty. It occurs within such English words as 'singer', but not at the beginning of English words. In the pronunciation of *nā* it will be found that the tongue presses firmly against the upper teeth and roof of the mouth. With *ngā*, by contrast, the tip of the tongue should be kept firmly behind the lower teeth, in the same position as for *kā*.

In fact, although many Māori words do begin with *ng*, in actual Māori speech or text (this does not apply when a Māori word is set in English text) the ng is always preceded by a vowel sound (e.g. *Ko ngā* ***tāngata ēnei***. — 'These are the people.')

The digraph *wh* was the last addition to the present alphabet, and is the most varied in sound value. In some areas a plain '*h*' will be heard; in other areas the sound is as in 'when'. The most widely taught pronunciation now is as a soft 'f' sound.

Several common words actually have alternative spellings with *h* and *wh*.

e.g. ***hea*** or ***whea*** for 'where?'
tēhea or ***tēwhea*** for 'which?'
pōhiri or ***pōwhiri*** (***-tia***) for 'to greet or beckon'

Stress

The main stress, or accent, in a word normally falls on the first long vowel, if there is one. If there is no long vowel, the stress usually falls on the first pair of vowels. If there are no vowel-pairs, the stress is usually on the first vowel, provided (as explained in *Let's Learn Maori*) this is not more than four vowels from the end of the word. The prefix ***whaka-*** is usually unstressed.

Stress is probably better considered in the context of whole phrases — since, as is emphasized in *Let's Learn Maori* (p. 17) the 'phrase, not the word, . . . is the natural pause unit of speech.' Advice on stress may be followed up in the same book (pp. 132-3).

It must be reiterated that the way to good pronunciation is through careful listening to good speakers, and much practice!

NOTES

1. The exact number of particles in Māori (or any other Polynesian language — as far as I know) has not yet been precisely determined. This is because some particles of similar sound are words of quite different functions, one from the other, and each such case must be counted as a separate word.
For example, *kei* as a location preposition (used also with *te* before verbs) must be considered as a distinctly separate word from *kei* as a verbal particle carrying the sense of a warning.
The concern here is solely with the functions of words in Māori (not with what English words may be used in translation: some Māori particles may require different translations in different contexts for what is only a single function in Māori). It is not always easy, however, to decide exactly what constitutes a discreetly different function in Māori.
In this book the total count of particles considered (including 3 different words for *a*, 3 for *e*, 3 for *i*, 2 for *kei*, 2 for *mā* and 3 for *me*) comes to fifty-three. Some slightly less common prepositions have not been included (e.g. *rā* — 'through', 'by way of' and *tō* — 'up to') nor have some variants (e.g. *koi/kei* — 'whilst' and *kai* as a dialectal variant of *kei*). Even apart from these omissions however, probably several further functions of words which are discussed could also be distinguished.

2. Adverbs (particularly those formed by adding '-ly' to adjectives) are usually considered as a fourth main class of base word in English. In traditional Latin grammar adverbs are considered to belong with the particles. Perhaps those adverbs in English which exist independently (i.e. are not formed by adding '-ly' to adjectives — e.g. 'here', 'very', 'upwards') should also be considered as particles. This situation seems to be complicated in English, however, by the fact that most such adverbs may also be used as adjectives. The situation in Māori is much simpler — with words such as *nei* (here) *rawa* (very) and *ake* (upwards)

being considered (in almost all their uses) as adverbial particles.

It is apparent, however, that even in Māori, the situation with 'adverb-type' words in general could well be further clarified. Most of these words follow the base word they qualify. Those which may be called 'manner particles' or 'adverbs of manner' (*kau, kē, koa, noa, pea, rawa, tonu*) usually follow the base directly (i.e. before any other particles — see *Let's Learn Maori*, pp. 69-71) and may also be given passive-endings (usually *-tia*) when following bases which are in the passive form.

At least two 'adverb-type' words to which this does not apply are ***āta*** (carefully) and ***mātua*** (first) in that, exceptionally (like the nouns ***tino*** and ***āhua***) they precede base words they qualify. ***Āta*** seems to be used only in such an adverbial sense, but ***mātua*** is used more variously, and is surely the same word as that used for 'parent' (***matua***, with its plural form ***mātua***)? It might be noted that ***tupuna*** (ancestor) may also be used preceding a noun it qualifies.

Confusion regarding adverbs is apparently nothing new among grammarians (or at least among 'learners'). The earliest use of the word 'adverb' recorded in *The Oxford English Dictionary* (from an English language grammar of French by John Palsgrave, published in 1530) is:

'It is harde to a lerner to discerne the difference bytwene an adverbe and other partes of spetche.'

3. Some words, it appears, exist in identical, or closely related, forms as both stative verbs and action verbs. e.g. ***pai*** as a stative verb meaning 'to be good' and ***pai*** (***-ngia***) as an action verb meaning 'to like'; ***pakaru*** as a stative verb meaning 'to be broken' and ***pākaru*** (***-a*** or ***-tia***) as an action verb meaning 'to break'. (Thus, in some contexts ***pākarutia*** may be presumed to have the same meaning as ***pakaru*** — but the preposition introducing an 'agent' should be *e* in the first case and *i* in the second. See pp. 92-94.)

There are, however, instances of words which may be considered to be stative verbs occurring with passive-endings. e.g. In Williams' dictionary under the entry for ***ngaro*** (to be missing, lost) may be found

ngaromia (quoted from *Ngā mahi a ngā tūpuna*) with the meaning given as 'be destroyed'. Under the entry for ***hinga*** may be found ***hingaia*** (be fallen upon).

For further reference to additional uses of passive endings page XXXVI of the introduction in Williams' dictionary may be consulted.

SELECTED BIBLIOGRAPHY

Dictionaries

MĀORI TO ENGLISH

Williams, Herbert W.
A DICTIONARY OF THE MAORI LANGUAGE
7th ed. Wellington, 1971.

On the back cover of the current (paperback, 1990) printing is an outline of the story of the development of this dictionary from its first edition in 1844 (1852, as printed, was actually the date of the second edition). This dictionary is not up-to-date, its grammar-basis could be re-vamped, and long vowels are not marked in the quotations which illustrate word-usage. Yet this is still a superb dictionary — particularly important for the care taken in choosing, and selecting from, its reference sources. By far the most important Māori to English reference.

Harlow, Ray
A WORD-LIST OF SOUTH ISLAND MĀORI
2nd revised edition Auckland, 1987

This is much more than a simple dictionary. Based on the vocabulary collection of Rev. James Watkin, Wesleyan minister at Waikouaiti 1840-44, and on other sources, it provides fascinating information on South Island dialect.

ENGLISH TO MĀORI

Ngata, H.M.
ENGLISH-MAORI DICTIONARY
Wellington, 1993.

Based on the Ngāti Porou dialect, this is another splendid dictionary in that it gives examples of usage in phrases and sentences. Appendix 1 consists of a helpful explanation (by Patu Hohepa) of the use of possessives; but in the body of the dictionary no references are made to grammatical terms. Instead, the correct words for given English contexts are simply shown by the example phrases. Frequently, of course, the Māori phrase has quite a different structure to the English. In this dictionary, also, the word *kai* is regularly used as the Ngāti Porou dialectal form for *kei*. An excellent companion volume to Williams' dictionary.

Biggs, Bruce
THE COMPLETE ENGLISH-MAORI DICTIONARY
Auckland, 1981.
In spite of the advent of the H.M. Ngata dictionary described above, this remains a most important finder-list for seeking Māori equivalents for English words. The Māori words must be cross-checked for usage with a native speaker or with Williams' dictionary. (It should be noted that in all of Bruce Biggs' books, for clearly argued reasons, long vowels are represented by doubling of the letter rather than by use of the macron.)

TWO-WAY DICTIONARIES

Ryan, P.M.
THE REED DICTIONARY OF MODERN MĀORI
Auckland, 1995.
This is now the most comprehensive and up-to-date dictionary available. It does not supply quotations illustrating usage, but even for classical Māori words it is invaluable for rapid reference.

Biggs, Bruce
ENGLISH • MĀORI MĀORI • ENGLISH DICTIONARY
Auckland, 1987.
This concise dictionary gives (in the English to Māori section) the part of speech (the word-type) of a good proportion of the Māori base words — an extremely useful feature, since this information tells exactly in which kinds of construction a word may be used.

Māori Language Commission/Te Taura Whiri i te Reo Māori
TE MATATIKI — CONTEMPORARY MĀORI WORDS
Auckland, 1996
An important reference of contemporary terminology in Māori, including many specialised terms for home, office, sports, science, medicine, and other fields.

Note: There is as yet no Māori dictionary available (i.e. a dictionary exclusively in Māori). The examples of usage in both Williams' dictionary and the H.M. Ngata dictionary may perhaps, to a limited extent, be used to supply this deficit.

Grammars and Courses

Only works currently in print are listed.
(AT) = accompanying audio-tapes are available.

Bauer, Winifred, with William Parker, Te Kareongawai Evans and Te Aroha Noti Teepa
THE REED REFERENCE GRAMMAR OF MĀORI
Auckland, 1997
This is the most comprehensive grammar of Māori ever published. It has been developed from, (and is more accessible than) the earlier *Māori* (1993) in the Routledge *Descriptive Grammars* series. It is unquestionably of primary importance to serious students of the grammar of Māori, but its insights must also be valuable for others.

Biggs, Bruce
LET'S LEARN MAORI
Auckland (rev. ed.) 1993.
The foundation of a grammar appropriate to the Māori language. (AT)

Foster, John
HE WHAKAMĀRAMA: A NEW COURSE IN MĀORI
Auckland, 1987.
A clearly written, progressive course with exercises (and answers) and a particularly useful chapter on the particle *ai*. (AT)

Harawira, K.T. revised by Tīmoti Kāretu
TEACH YOURSELF MĀORI
Auckland, 1994.
Somehow, quite astonishingly, this book manages to contain the essentials of Māori grammar (including details of the uses of *ko, ai* and *anō*) along with exercises, answers and a 38 page vocabulary — all in a pocket-size format.

Head, Lyndsay
MAKING MAORI SENTENCES
Auckland, 1989.
Detailed analysis of phrase and sentence structure, showing how sentences may be built up. Some very useful sections.

Kāretu, T.S.
TE REO RANGATIRA: A COURSE IN MĀORI FOR SIXTH AND SEVENTH FORMS.
Wellington (reprinted) 1984.
This is in similar format to, and constitutes an excellent continuation of, the *Te Rangatahi* series (see Waititi below). It is more up-to-date. (Tūhoe dialect.)

Moorfield, John C.
TE WHANAKE 1: TE KĀKANO Auckland, 1988.
TE WHANAKE 2: TE PIHINGA Auckland, 1989.
TE WHANAKE 3: TE MĀHURI Auckland, 1992.
This is now the first choice for a comprehensive course at university level. 'It is . . . not a self-tutor, but rather should accompany classroom activities designed to develop learners' communicative competence.' (See back cover of *Te Kākano*.) (AT)

Ryan, P.M.
MODERN MĀORI, BOOK ONE Auckland, 1978.
MODERN MĀORI, BOOK TWO Auckland, 1980.
These books form a most readable course, with a variety of exercises including poems, speeches, action songs and crosswords.

Tauroa, Patricia
THE COLLINS MAORI PHRASE BOOK
Auckland, 1990.
Contains an excellent selection of phrases and expressions for use in a wide variety of situations.

Waititi, Hoani R.
TE RANGATAHI, ELEMENTARY 1 Rev. ed. Wellington, 1970.
TE RANGATAHI, ELEMENTARY 2 Rev. ed. Wellington, 1972.
TE RANGATAHI, ELEMENTARY 3 Rev. ed. Wellington, 1985.
The *Te Rangatahi* series has been subjected to the criticism that its content is out-of-date, its 'political correctness' questionable (boys hunt pigs, girls do the cooking) and for the use of English borrowings in place of genuine Māori words (e.g. *māmā* instead of *whaea*). Whatever the validity of these criticisms, the format and methodology of this course remain (in my view) as yet unsurpassed. Although it may be used as a self-tutor, like *Te Whanake* it is really designed for use in a group with a teacher (answers to the exercises are not provided).

The series has had quite a complicated publishing history, much of the material having been revised and re-edited (by Mrs Beth Ranapia). The three books in the *Elementary* series, as listed, would now seem to be the preferred version (which may be followed, as noted above, by Tīmoti Kāretu's *Te Reo Rangatira*). (AT)

(The audio-tapes relating to the *Te Rangatahi* series have the title *He Awhina*. This large set of tapes, and the set for the *Te Whanake* series, are expensive, but may be accessed at universities and perhaps other institutions.)

Texts of Major Historical Importance

Much Māori writing of last century remains in manuscripts, awaiting publication, and previously published material, such as that in John White's six volumes of *The Ancient History of the Māori* (1887-90) is out of print and generally accessible only at a few libraries.

A reprint is at present under consideration for *Ngā Mahi a Ngā Tūpuna* — the compilation of prose narratives of mythology originally edited by George Grey in the middle of last century. Last printed in 1971, this book (along with Grey's English rendering in *Polynesian Mythology*) has long held centre-stage as a printed repository of the most widely popularized versions of several myths. Put together by Grey from contributions by several different Māori writers, it represents only a fraction of his collection of around 10,000 pages of manuscripts now held at the Auckland Public Library. (See D.R. Simmons' 'The Sources of Sir George Grey's *Ngā Mahi a Ngā Tūpuna*' in *The Journal of the Polynesian Society*, vol. 75, no. 2, June 1966.)

One of the foremost contributors to Grey's collection was the Arawa chief Te Rangikāheke. His own version (rather than Grey's edited version) of the Māui stories has now been made available as follows:

Te Rangikāheke
THE STORY OF MĀUI
Christchurch, 1992.
Edited with translation and commentary by Agathe Thornton.

Two other volumes of significant variant traditions in mythology have also been published in recent years:

Ruatapu, Mohi
NGĀ KŌRERO A MOHI RUATAPU, TOHUNGA RONGONUI O NGĀTI POROU:
The writings of Mohi Ruatapu; translated, edited and annotated by Anaru Reedy. Christchurch, 1993.
Nga Kōrero a Mohi Ruatapu is an excellent edition of two manuscripts, dating from 1871 and 1875 respectively.

Tiramōrehu, Matiaha
TE: WAIATATANGA MAI O TE ATUA: South Island traditions recorded by Matiaha Tiramōrehu; edited by Manu van Ballekom and Ray Harlow. Christchurch, 1987.
The material of this 1849 manuscript was used (without accreditation to the author) in the first volume of White's *The Ancient History of the Māori*. Now it is restored to its correct order (see the introduction).

The following four volumes comprise the paramount collection of Māori poetry:

Ngata, A.T. and Pei Te Hurunui
NGĀ MŌTEATEA (PART 1).
Facsimile of the Wellington 1959 edition, with a new introduction by Wharetoroa Kerr. 1988.

Ngata, A.T. and Pei Te Hurunui
NGĀ MŌTEATEA (PART 2). Facsimile of the Wellington 1961 edition, with a new foreword by Ray Harlow. 1986.

Ngata, A.T. and Pei Te Hurunui
NGĀ MŌTEATEA (PART 3). Facsimile of the Wellington 1970 edition. 1980.

Ngata, A.T.
NGĀ MŌTEATEA (PART 4). Auckland, 1990.

The Polynesian Society is committed to keeping these books in print (see Ray Harlow's foreword to Part 2). Most of the songs require some understanding of historical events or circumstances to which they relate. Notes are provided in Māori in all four volumes, and in the first three volumes English translations are provided for both songs and notes. Further explication of some songs may be found (with music) in:

McLean, Mervyn and Margaret Orbell
TRADITIONAL SONGS OF THE MĀORI
Auckland, 1975.

The kinds of sayings called *pepeha, whakataukī* and *whakatauāki* (often, in English, called 'proverbs') form a major literary genre in Māori. A collection more comprehensive than any previously published is progressively being issued by the Department of Māori Studies of Victoria University of Wellington. The arrangement is alphabetical (by first letter of the opening word). Volumes so far published are:

Mead, H. Moko and Neil Grove (i kohikohi)
NGA PEPEHA A NGA TŪPUNA: TE WĀHANGA 1 (A AND E) 1989.
NGA PEPEHA A NGA TŪPUNA: TE WĀHANGA 2 (H) 1991.
NGA PEPEHA A NGA TŪPUNA: TE WĀHANGA 3 (I AND K) 1994.

Although a translation, the Māori Bible is undoubtedly a significant text. It has recently been re-issued by Te Pīhopatanga o Aotearoa, edited by Cleve Barlow in an excellent bilingual format with the 'King James' English version (which it closely parallels) as:

KO TE PAIPERA TAPU: THE HOLY BIBLE (Rotorua, 1992).

Recent Books in Māori

It was intended to confine this bibliography to currently available books specifically to do with language (with the inclusion of some historically significant texts). But all books are 'to do with language', and mention must be made of the range of children's books issued particularly during the past decade or so, including the recent *Te mātāwai* series.

The last few years have also seen the appearance of full-length works in various fields — important not only for their subject-content but also because they are setting contemporary standards for written (and printed) Māori. (It could be noted that consensus has not yet been reached as to how vowel-length should be indicated.) A list of such books would include Ruka Broughton's *Ngaa mahi whakaari a Tiitokowaru* (1993), Hēmi Pōtatau's *He hokinga mahara* (1991), the collection of *Nga kōrero a Reweti Kohere mā* (1994), Cleve Barlow's bilingual *Tikanga whakaaro* (1991) and (1995) *Nga Iwi o Tainui* by Pei Te Hurunui Jones and Bruce Biggs.

A high literary standard is also a feature of the currently appearing major reference work of Māori language versions of the biographies of Māori people in *The Dictionary of New Zealand Biography*. Two volumes have so far been published:

NGĀ TĀNGATA TAUMATA RAU 1769-1869. Wellington, 1990.

NGĀ TĀNGATA TAUMATA RAU 1870-1900. Wellington, 1994.

(The English versions of these volumes are titled, respectively, *The People of Many Peaks* and *The Turbulent Years*.)

English Grammar

Hurford, James R.
GRAMMAR: A STUDENTS GUIDE
Cambridge, 1994.

Out of a situation which has frequently seemed to be increasingly confusing comes this book of remarkable clarity and order. The arrangement is alphabetical (by topic) and exercises (with answers) are included. The value of comparison between languages is also appreciated. An excellent reference.

Index of Particles

For particles in general see also Note 1, pg 118

Index of Grammatical Terms

(Chapter 28 — Summarizing — has not been included)